HOW PSYCHOLOGISTS DO RESEARCH
The Example of Anxiety

PRENTICE-HALL SERIES IN EXPERIMENTAL PSYCHOLOGY

James J. Jenkins, Editor

HOW PSYCHOLOGISTS DO RESEARCH

The Example of Anxiety

DAVID S. DUSTIN
State University of New York, Plattsburgh

PRENTICE-HALL, INC., ENGLEWOOD CLIFFS, N.J.

PRENTICE-HALL INTERNATIONAL, INC., *London*
PRENTICE-HALL OF AUSTRALIA, PTY. LTD., *Sydney*
PRENTICE-HALL OF CANADA, LTD., *Toronto*
PRENTICE-HALL OF INDIA PRIVATE LTD., *New Delhi*
PRENTICE-HALL OF JAPAN, INC., *Tokyo*

© 1969

PRENTICE-HALL, INC., ENGLEWOOD CLIFFS, N.J.

Current printing (last digit):
10 9 8 7 6 5 4 3

Library of Congress Catalog Card Number: 69-12973

PRINTED IN THE UNITED STATES OF AMERICA

Preface

This book is based on two main assumptions:

1. Even the beginner in psychology should learn something about research. Otherwise, his impression of what psychologists do cannot be very complete. Otherwise, too, he may place excessive confidence in psychological principles, not realizing that the research from which they stem is fallible.

2. A particularly effective and interesting way of conveying this information is to show research techniques being used in actual studies. For the sake of continuity, it seemed desirable that all the illustrative studies be relevant to the same topic. The topic chosen was anxiety.

The even-numbered chapters in this book describe examples of various types of research: Chapter 2, an exploratory study (by Freud); Chapter 4, an example of test development (by the Thurstones and Willoughby); Chapter 6, a sample survey (by the Survey Research Center); Chapter 8, experiments (by Pavlov and Neal Miller); Chapter 10, more experiments (by Mowrer and Solomon); and Chapter 12, work culminating in one brand of behavior therapy (by Watson, Mary Cover Jones, and Wolpe). Following each descriptive chapter is a chapter which elaborates on the methods used and evaluates them.

My major goal has been to present briefly and clearly a rather complete set of methodological principles. I have *not* attempted to:

1. Present the methods in enough detail to allow the reader to apply them with any sophistication.

2. Write a comprehensive survey of research on anxiety. Even the few studies that are presented are, in most cases, greatly abbreviated.

3. Make the methodological evaluations at all complete. In each case, I have

mentioned only selected illustrations of major methodological issues—primarily the issues of accuracy of measurement, generalizability, and causality.

I am grateful for the assistance of many persons. My editor, James J. Jenkins, encouraged and greatly helped me to realize this somewhat untried idea for a book. My colleagues Edwin I. Megargee, Louis J. Moran, Henry C. Morlock, and Noel W. Smith read selected chapters and directed my attention to relevant studies and methodological points that I had overlooked. My wife, Jeanne A. Dustin, expertly read the entire manuscript for clarity and style. Finally, Miss Linda A. Rosselli capably assisted with the typing.

DAVID S. DUSTIN

Contents

HOW PSYCHOLOGISTS DO RESEARCH
The Example of Anxiety

1 Introduction

This book presents and discusses some investigations which psychologists have carried out on the topic of anxiety. Before progressing to specific instances of investigation, however, we shall need to give some tentative answers to two questions which naturally arise at the outset: What is anxiety? What are the principles of psychological investigation?

WHAT IS ANXIETY?

To help us understand anxiety, we will first describe a related emotion—fear. Fear is an emotion produced by danger. As the danger increases, so does the fear. Taking a driving test, interviewing for a job, or walking down an unlighted street at night may produce some fear, but it will be easily controlled. As the danger increases, however, symptoms such as pounding of the heart, a sinking feeling in the stomach, shaking and trembling, and cold sweat become more difficult to control. In extreme fear, or panic, thought deteriorates into a nightmare of distorted mental images, and the person may run wildly about, crying, shouting, and laughing in rapid succession. Though you have probably experienced panic, you may not recall just how excruciatingly unpleasant it was because it is usually forgotten soon after the crisis is over.

Fear is natural in dangerous situations and so is not puzzling to us. But if these same emotional reactions occur when there is not enough danger to warrant them, these same emotions are called anxiety, and they are very puzzling indeed.

One example of a severe attack of anxiety is described in the autobiography of William Ellery Leonard,[1] for many years a professor of English at the University of Wisconsin. One day when he was 35 he went for a walk in the woods and eventually came to a lonely bluff overlooking a lake near Madison, Wisconsin. While standing there, he began to feel uneasy; he took off his hat, mopped his head, and fanned his face. Suddenly a freight train appeared on the tracks across the lake, blowing its whistle. Instantly panic set in. According to Leonard, he was immediately overwhelmed by a feeling of acute danger and he soon found himself running back and forth on the bluff, shouting, and smashing a wooden box he had found nearby into small pieces.

It is puzzling behavior like this that leads to research. How research can help to explain such behavior is described later in this chapter.

Anxiety, particularly when extreme, is considered a "sick" or maladjusted reaction. In fact, it is generally thought to be the basis of the psychoneuroses, those psychological maladjustments that may involve such symptoms as anxiety, phobia, depression, amnesia, obsession, compulsion, and physical complaints having no physiological basis. Many of these symptoms occur in mild form in normal persons; it is only when they become seriously disabling that they are considered neurotic. Anxiety is currently thought to be the most basic of these neurotic symptoms: it is the first to occur and is so unpleasant that the other symptoms develop partly as attempts to avoid or bury the anxiety.

Most of the anxieties described in this book are phobias, that is, anxieties focused on a specific class of stimuli—whether it be snakes, heights, crowds, locomotives, or virtually anything else. Even though phobias—unlike other anxieties—are attached to known stimuli, they still classify as anxieties because the stimuli to which they are attached are not dangerous enough to justify the amount of emotion shown.

INVESTIGATION: THREE KINDS
OF NEEDED EVIDENCE

The question raised by Leonard's panic is this: Why was this grown man so frightened of a train which, being separated from him by a half mile of water, could not possibly harm him? In this book we will explore the major kinds of evidence needed to explain such puzzles and the major techniques the psychologist uses to gather this evidence.

If, in attempting to answer this question, we delved into Leonard's

[1] *The Locomotive-God* (New York: The Century Co., 1927).

life history, we would find that in his childhood a locomotive nearly ran him down. This might lead us to guess that this early experience had taught him to fear locomotives and that this fear continued into adulthood. Furthermore, not being satisfied with specific explanations of specific events, we might go on to suggest that this is only one instance of a more general principle. We might theorize, for example, that learning causes anxiety.

This brief attempt to explain Leonard's locomotive phobia has, in crude form, the basic ingredients of a psychological research. The goal of research is to explain adequately as many important facts as possible. Three main steps lead to this goal: measurement, inferring causality, and generalization. Weakness at any one of these steps will weaken the conclusions that may be drawn from a study.

①

Measurement. Researchers make observations or measurements of variables they consider interesting or important. A *variable* is any characteristic that may vary in amount or degree. The world the psychologist studies is composed mainly of *stimuli* (parts of the environment), *subjects* (observed organisms), and *responses* (subjects' behavioral reactions). Therefore psychologists are concerned mainly with stimulus variables, such as the distance of a locomotive, the loudness of its whistle, and the length of time it is visible; subject variables, such as a person's age, the accuracy of his memory, and the intensity of his internal emotions; and response variables, such as rate of heartbeat or degree to which behavior is disorganized.

Anxiety can be considered a subject variable. However, one cannot observe anxiety itself. One can observe only trembling, perspiring, and other external manifestations of anxiety. For research purposes, then, anxiety and many other subject variables must be translated into measurable response variables.

The accuracy of a psychological measure is often broken down into two parts: its *reliability* and its *validity*. A test is reliable to the extent that a subject's scores on two administrations of that test are consistent. Since the test stimulus, the instructions, the method of responding, and the method used to score the responses can affect test scores, reliability is likely to be higher when these extraneous variables are not permitted to change from one administration of the test to another. Whereas reliability concerns the degree to which a test is measuring anything consistently, validity concerns what a test is measuring. A test is valid to the extent that it measures what it is supposed to measure.

The conclusions drawn from a study can hardly be accurate if its measurements are inaccurate. For example, our information about Leonard's behavior would certainly not be any evidence for the theory that "Learning causes anxiety" if the report of his shouting, rushing about, and breaking a box was not an accurate measure of anxiety. Perhaps, for example, his reported behavior reflected anger, not anxiety, or perhaps he was merely rehearsing a part for a play. To help the researcher avoid this kind of error, methods are available for determining whether a measuring instrument has the required degree of reliability and validity.

②**Inferring causality.** The researcher's next step after measurement is often that of theorizing about causality. For example, we guessed that it was Leonard's childhood encounter with a locomotive which caused him to be anxious when the train appeared across the lake. This is not to claim, by the way, that this experience is the only cause of his anxiety, or that it always causes him to be anxious of trains. The word "cause," as ordinarily used in psychology, need mean only that one variable sometimes affects another to some extent.

In our statement "Learning causes anxiety," anxiety would be called the *dependent variable* because it is thought to depend on (to be caused by) past learning; learning would be called the *independent variable*. Variables that the researcher wishes to clear out of the way so that they cannot confuse his study of the independent and dependent variables may be called *extraneous variables*.

Our conclusion that "Learning causes anxiety" would not be warranted by this study if our inferences about causality were incorrect. Perhaps, for example, we overlooked some extraneous variable like insecurity which was the true cause of Leonard's anxiety attack. To help the researcher avoid this kind of error, methods are available for guarding against the possibility that extraneous variables are influencing dependent variables in a study.

③**Generalization.** Another step the researcher often takes in explaining observations is that of generalizing a causal relationship to stimuli, subjects, and responses beyond the specific ones used in his study. We carried this to an extreme by suggesting that "All kinds of learning cause all organisms to make all anxiety responses"—in short, that "Learning causes anxiety." Such statements are theories or parts of theories.

A *theory* is an abstract generalization about the nature of reality. The more general the theory, the greater number of specific events it explains. Most theories partly summarize available evidence and partly go beyond it to predict new events. Theories for which evidence is incomplete—such as our theory that "Learning causes anxiety"—are called *hypotheses*. Later, if such theories continue to survive research tests until the evidence for them becomes virtually complete, they are called *laws*. Psychology has many hypotheses but few laws.

Generalization, too, must be accurate. Even if it is true that Leonard's early experience with the locomotive caused his panic on the bluff, this fact does not necessarily mean that all instances of learning cause all kinds of organisms to show all kinds of anxiety responses, as our theory states. Leonard's case may be unique, following principles that do not apply to other stimuli, subjects, and responses. Fortunately, there are methods the researcher may use to ensure that the generalizations he wishes to make will be justified.

Measurement, causality, and generalization, then, are the main issues about which the researcher tries to gather evidence. The methods available for gathering these kinds of evidence are described in the following section.

INVESTIGATION: METHODS OF GATHERING THE NEEDED EVIDENCE

Perhaps the most basic tools of psychological research are three principles about causation.[2] Although the most obvious application of these principles is to the problem of inferring causality, some of them are also used to attack the problems of measurement and generalization.

PRINCIPLE 1: *If differences on one variable occur where there are also differences on another, one of the two variables might be directly causing the other.* Leonard had had a more frightening experience with a locomotive than with anything else and he now showed more anxiety toward locomotives than toward anything else. In other words, his learning differed with respect to locomotives and other stimuli, and so did his anxiety. Such variables are said to be *related*.

Logic says that one of two related variables might be directly causing the other. However, two other possibilities also exist. For one thing, it might be purely coincidental that Leonard's learning and his anxiety were related. We could rule out this explanation by showing that learning is consistently related to anxiety. Another possibility is that the two related variables are causally linked only indirectly, through some extraneous variable. For example, perhaps the childhood experience with the locomotive, since it occurred when Leonard strayed from his parents at the railroad station, made him extremely afraid of being left alone. Perhaps, then, because he happened to associate trains—as well as automobiles, luggage, etc.—with the idea of his parents and friends leaving him alone, he became anxious about them. If this was the case, the locomo-

---

[2] A classic version of these principles may be found in E. Nagel, ed., *John Stuart Mill's Philosophy of Scientific Method* (New York: Hafner Publishing Co., Inc., 1950).

tive phobia was caused, not by the childhood experience itself, but by the general insecurity that had been caused by that experience.

The way to rule out the possibility that extraneous variables are responsible for an obtained relationship is to eliminate differences on them. In our example, we might measure Leonard's anxiety toward locomotives and toward other objects once again, this time making sure that he felt equally secure during both measurements. This method is based on Principle 2, which is discussed in more detail later.

The researcher uses Principle 1 by finding or creating a difference on the independent variable, then looking for differences on the dependent variable. He can obtain groups of subjects which differ on a stimulus, subject, or response variable by either of the following methods:

1. *Manipulating* the variable—that is to say, creating differences on it. For example, an investigator studying the effects of learning on anxiety might try to instill anxiety in one group of subjects but not in another.

   Although there is no upper limit on the number of different groups of subjects that may be used in this kind of study, the minimum is usually two —sometimes called the experimental group and the control group. By later comparing the mean[3] amount of anxiety shown to locomotives by the experimental group, which was trained to fear them, with that shown by the control group, which received no such training, the effect of learning on anxiety could be discovered. A study in which the independent variable is manipulated is called an *experimental study,* or an experiment.

2. Making use of *natural variation*—for example, measuring subjects on the variable, then considering those scoring high as one group and those scoring low as another. A researcher using this method would not try to change his subjects' experiences with locomotives, for example. Instead, he would find out which subjects had already—in the natural courses of their lives—been terrified by locomotives and which had not. The mean anxiety these two groups showed to locomotives would then be compared to see if anxiety was related to learning. This would be a *non-experimental study.*

PRINCIPLE 2: *If differences on one variable occur where there are no differences on another, neither variable can possibly be causing the other.* This principle is the complement of the first. It is most often applied by preventing differences from occurring on (that is, by "controlling") extraneous variables while the independent variable varies, then looking to see if a difference appears on the dependent variable. If it does appear, it can't be due to the controlled variables. And if the researcher could ever be certain that he had completely controlled all influential extraneous variables, he would know that the obtained difference was entirely due

---

[3] The *mean* of a group of scores is the sum of those scores divided by the number of scores. It is what the layman usually calls "the average." For the psychologist, however, the mean is only one of several kinds of average.

to the independent variable. Unfortunately, however, the researcher never can be certain of this.

In our imaginary study on anxiety learning, suppose we decided that the size of the locomotive used in measuring anxiety reactions and the age of the subjects were important extraneous variables to control since they both could affect the amount of anxiety shown. These two variables will now be used to illustrate the three major methods of controlling a variable:

1. *Holding* the variable *constant,* or creating similarity on it. A researcher could hold constant the size of the locomotive used in the measurement of locomotive phobia by presenting exactly the same locomotive to both the trained and untrained subjects.

   Subject variables, too, can be held constant if the very same subjects can be used in both experimental and control conditions. In terms of our example, the same subjects might learn anxiety one month and unlearn their anxiety the next. This is called "using the subject as his own control" and usually results in very exact control of all subject variables.

2. *Matching,* or measuring subjects on a variable and then assigning them to the different groups in such a way that all groups have equivalent mean scores on that variable. One way to match on age would be to find out the age of each trained and each untrained subject, then to omit enough older subjects from one group and/or younger subjects from the other to make the two groups equal in mean age.

3. *Randomization,* or splitting a group (often called a *population*) of subjects (or stimuli or responses) into subgroups (often called *samples*) in a random way. Randomization is used sometimes to select a sample of subjects from a larger population, sometimes to divide the selected subjects into experimental and control groups.

   A procedure for assigning subjects to groups is random if it gives each subject an equal opportunity to fall into each group. To control subject age by randomization, one would pay no attention to age or to any other subject variable. Instead, which of our two groups each subject was assigned to would depend only, let us say, on whether a coin landed heads or tails.

   The reason randomization results in equivalent groups is roughly as follows: while the random fall of the coin might first put an older subject in one group and a younger in the other, eventually it would balance things out by assigning a younger subject to the first group and an older to the second. The greater the number of subjects who are run through the random assignment mill, the more opportunity there is for this kind of balancing to occur.

   Although randomization tends to provide better control the larger the number of subjects used, it seldom reaches the degree of control offered by the techniques of holding constant or matching. However, this disadvantage is offset by the fact that randomization controls *all* subject variables. In the above example, it was not only subjects' age that was being balanced out; at the same time, the same process was occurring for subjects' sex, their previous anxiety learning, their height, and every other subject variable.

The researcher can match on variables and hold variables constant in both experimental and non-experimental studies. However, completely random assignment of subjects is possible only in an experiment. This is because in an experiment differences on the independent variable are produced by manipulation, which needn't interfere with random assignment. In a non-experimental study, however, the independent variable must be varied by assigning particular kinds of subjects to particular groups—a procedure which is not at all random.

When combined, our first two principles tell us that if two variables are related when most influential extraneous variables are controlled, then one of the two is probably causing the other. But it is not always obvious which is cause and which is effect. For example, suppose that a person who once stalled his car on a railroad track and was grazed by a train now becomes anxious whenever he sees a locomotive. It could be that the accident caused the anxiety, but it is also possible that a strong anxiety about trains was what made him stall on the tracks in the first place. To find out what is cause and what is effect, the researcher may turn to a third principle.

PRINCIPLE 3: *If two variables are directly causally related, it is the one on which differences occur first that is causing the obtained differences on the other.*

In the experimental study it is always clear upon which variable differences occurred first. It has to be the independent variable, the one the experimenter manipulated.

It is usually not so clear upon which variable differences occurred first in the non-experimental study. The researcher may see that two variables show differences, but he doesn't know which one varied first. While common sense may favor one particular causal relationship, it usually cannot completely rule out others.

Now let us summarize the nature of research. The investigator observes a relatively uninformative or ambiguous set of events (e.g., Leonard's behavior when the locomotive appeared), wonders why they occurred, and forms a theoretical explanation of them (e.g., "Learning causes anxiety"). Then, realizing that his theory lacks evidence for accuracy of measurement, causality, and generalizability, he seeks ways to gather the needed evidence. Using the three logical principles presented in this chapter, the researcher would then design a new study in which he would observe more informative events. These new observations would lead to a theory which—whether it was the same as before or different—would have a greater likelihood of being correct because it would be based on more adequate information.

This picture of research as a sequence of observation-theory-observation-theory and so on, constantly producing ever more informative observations and ever more certain theories, is highly idealized. A more realistic view of the research process, with all its fits and starts, will be conveyed in this book by the descriptions of some investigations that have actually been carried out on anxiety and related topics.

2 Freud Explores the Nonsense of Little Hans

In medical school Sigmund Freud had specialized in neurology, spending long hours bent over a dissecting microscope exploring the nervous systems of specimens. Now that he was in private medical practice in Vienna, persons complaining of "nervous" or neurotic symptoms arrived at his office in the belief that neurology could help them. They were mistaken. At that time, neither neurology nor any other field of knowledge could provide much understanding of neurotic disorders. This did not discourage Freud, however. He accepted neurotic patients and set out to explore their problems through what was perhaps the most obvious method—he had patients tell about their symptoms and the events related to them. According to one biographer, "He felt sure there were many secrets hidden behind the manifest symptoms [of neurotic disorders], and his restless imagination burned to penetrate them."[1] He spent the rest of his life in these pioneering investigations and discovered many of the puzzles which continue to stimulate research today. Two of those puzzles—the relationship between anxiety and conflict, and that between anxiety and repression—are emphasized in this chapter. Later chapters describe more recent work on these two topics.

[1] E. Jones, *The Life and Work of Sigmund Freud*, I (New York: Basic Books, Inc., Publishers, 1953), 239.

FREUD'S EARLY OBSERVATIONS AND THEORIES

Freud began early to develop the notion that conflict is closely related to anxiety. One of the most anxiety-producing conflicts he noticed in his neurotic patients involved the Oedipus complex. Another important relationship he noticed was that between anxiety and repression. Here, there arose the question of whether anxiety causes repression, or repression causes anxiety. These early observations will now be described in more detail.

Conflict. Listening to neurotic adults trace the sources of their afflictions, Freud was surprised to find that, when the search was pursued long enough, it often led back to childhood conflicts that seemed partly sexual in nature. A prime example was the Oedipal conflict. A boy in the throes of this conflict apparently experiences strong "sexual" attraction toward his mother and jealousy of his father. In conflict with these tabooed feelings, Freud observed, is the boy's fear that his father will punish him for them. This conflict Freud called the Oedipus complex, after the mythical Greek who unwittingly killed his father and married his mother.

Freud found evidence for the existence of the Oedipus complex not only in the recollections of his patients, but also in his own self-analysis. Early in his career Freud had decided that he could learn more about the mind by exploring his own; thenceforth he had devoted the last half hour of every day to analyzing himself. Later he wrote to a friend: "I have found love of the mother and jealousy of the father in my own case too, and now believe it to be a general phenomenon of early childhood. . . ."[2]

Such observations led Freud to the theory that every boy at some time in his childhood experiences the Oedipal conflict. Furthermore, Freud thought, this conflict produces in the boy a great deal of anxiety. It is important to notice, however, that he was basing this theory on the memories of adults, which might have been faulty. For this reason, Freud was eager to test his theory through direct observation of children.

Repression. Even though the Oedipal conflict seemed to lie at the root of the neuroses of many of his male patients, Freud thought the same conflict had also been experienced by normal, non-neurotic men. Apparently conflict leads to adult neurosis under some conditions, but not under

2 Sigmund Freud, *The Origins of Psycho-analysis*, letters to Wilhelm Fliess, drafts and notes: 1887–1902 (New York: Basic Books, Inc., Publishers, 1954; London: The Hogarth Press Ltd., 1954), p. 223.

others. What might the crucial condition be? Freud decided it was repression; any conflict, he hypothesized, would produce anxiety if it were
repressed.

The concept of repression arose from the difficulty Freud had had un-
covering crucial childhood memories of neurotic patients; only by the
greatest persistence and patience had he been able gradually to break
through patients' resistance to remembering such events. Why this inability to remember? It could not be that these events were forgotten due
to their unimportance; on the contrary, they were of the greatest importance. Freud decided that such memories had been repressed—
unwittingly "pushed" out of consciousness into the unconscious—because
they were too painful to think about. This kind of forgetting is clearly
illustrated in the case of a young governess whom Freud called Miss
Lucy R.:

> FREUD: I believe that really you are in love with your employer. . . .
> LUCY: Yes, I think that's true.
> FREUD: But if you knew you loved your employer why didn't you tell me?
> LUCY: I didn't know—or rather I didn't want to know. I wanted to drive it
> out of my head and not think of it again; and I believe latterly [lately] I
> have suceeded.[3]

Freud noticed that when patients' repressed memories were brought
back to consciousness, their anxiety often seemed to diminish. These
observations led him to the theory that repression causes anxiety. Like all
hypotheses, this one called for additional evidence.

In accord with this hypothesis, Freud attempted to cure his patients by
removing their repressions, thereby (if his hypothesis was correct) reducing
their anxiety. The method of psychotherapy which Freud developed on
the basis of this principle is called psychoanalysis and is still used today
by psychoanalysts.

THE CASE OF LITTLE HANS[4]

Mainly to gather more direct evidence for his theories about childhood,

[3] Josef Breuer and Sigmund Freud, *Studies on Hysteria* (New York: Basic Books,
Inc., Publishers, 1957), p. 117. This passage can also be found in J. Strachey, ed., *The
Standard Edition of the Complete Psychological Works of Sigmund Freud,* II (London:
The Hogarth Press Ltd., 1955), 117.

[4] The material in this section is based largely on Sigmund Freud, "Analysis of a
Phobia in a Five-Year-Old-Boy," in *Collected Papers of Sigmund Freud,* III (New
York: Basic Books, Inc., Publishers, 1959), 147–289. Also in J. Strachey, ed., *The Stand-
ard Edition of the Complete Psychological Works of Sigmund Freud,* X (London: The
Hogarth Press Ltd., 1955), 3–149.

Freud suggested to his friends and followers that they make careful observations of children. One result of this suggestion was a long series of reports on "Little Hans," written by Hans' father, a Viennese physician and a follower of Freud.

Hans' Oedipal conflict. Four-year-old Hans spent the summer of 1907 in a resort town far from Vienna. There he had many playmates and several "girl friends." There, also, he enjoyed the undivided attention of his mother during those parts of the summer when his father had business in Vienna. Sometimes, even—especially when Hans was anxious about going to bed at night—his mother would let him sleep in her bed.

But all this companionship ceased when the summer ended and the family returned to Vienna. Here, they had recently moved into a larger apartment, in a new neighborhood. This meant that Hans had no friends nearby to play with, and that he could have his own bedroom, instead of sleeping in his parents' bedroom as he used to do. Furthermore, Hans' father was more in evidence: now when Hans would ask to get in his mother's bed in the morning, his father would protest that it shouldn't be permitted. In the place of all the summer companionship, Hans had little more than a daily walk with his nursemaid, or sometimes his mother, through the city streets to the park or the zoo.

It was on one of those walks that Hans had an experience which Freud later interpreted as the immediate, exciting cause of Hans' neurosis. A horse fell down in the street and wildly thrashed its hoofs about, greatly frightening Hans.

Soon afterward, Hans' "nonsense," as Hans called it, began. One day en route to the park he suddenly began to cry and to ask to go home. He explained that he was afraid a horse would bite him. Thus began a phobia of horses which was to last the next four months. During that period Hans at times could bring himself to venture into the street when his father was with him and when few horses were about. At other times he would not go beyond his front door. Occasionally he said he was afraid a horse would come right into his room and bite him.

Hans' behavior naturally perplexed and worried his parents. So one Monday afternoon Hans and his father went to see Professor Freud. He showed them into the consulting room, closed the double doors, and pulled the heavy curtain over them. Then, undoubtedly puffing on a cigar, Freud listened while Hans told how he was afraid of horses, and especially bothered "by what horses wear in front of their eyes and by the black round their mouths."[5]

Freud described his own reactions on that occasion as follows:

[5] Freud, *Collected Papers,* III, 184; and Strachey, *Standard Edition,* X, 41.

As I saw the two of them sitting in front of me and at the same time heard Hans's description of his anxiety-horses, a further piece of the solution shot through my mind, and a piece which I could well understand might escape his father. I asked Hans jokingly whether his horses wore eyeglasses, to which he replied that they did not. I then asked him whether his father wore eyeglasses, to which, against all the evidence, he once more said no. Finally I asked him, whether by the "black round the mouth" he meant a moustache. . . .[6]

Thus the similarity between the father's glasses and mustache, and what were perhaps the feared horses' blinders and muzzles, suggested to Freud that Hans was really afraid of his father. This fear, when added to Freud's observation that Hans was "in love with" his mother, completed the picture of an Oedipal conflict. The finding of such a conflict in a patient suffering phobic anxiety seemed to support Freud's hypothesis that conflict is related to anxiety.

Hans' repression. The reason Hans' fear of his father was not apparent on the surface was, Freud thought, that he had repressed the conflict of which this fear was a part. However, repressed fear does not simply vanish, according to Freud; just as a dammed river finds a new channel, so repressed impulses find other, less direct expression. Hans' repressed fear of his father was expressed toward horses.

Why horses? Freud thought there were multiple reasons for this, as for most things the mind does. First, the previous summer Hans had heard it said to a person who was going away in a carriage: "Don't put your finger to the white horse or it'll bite you."[7] In this way, biting horses became associated with the idea of people going away, in Hans' mind. The idea of going away, in turn, he associated with his father because he wished his father would go away and leave him and his mother alone. Through these two associations, Freud thought, the father had become indirectly linked to biting horses in Hans' mind.

A second link was the similarity between the horses' blinders and muzzles and the father's glasses and mustache. These two links, Freud thought, were what caused the incident of the falling horse to stir up Hans' feelings toward his father.

This remained Freud's explanation of Hans' horse phobia, even though an attempt by Hans' father to verify this explanation by a direct question produced a rather uncertain answer:

[6] Freud, *Collected Papers,* III, 184; and Strachey, *Standard Edition,* X, 42.
[7] Freud, *Collected Papers,* III, 172; and Strachey, *Standard Edition,* X, 29.

FATHER: When the horse fell down, did you think of your daddy?
HANS: Perhaps. Yes. It's possible.[8]

Little Hans, then, was one of many patients in whom Freud thought he observed two things existing together: (1) anxiety, and (2) repression. As previously indicated, it was Freud's early guess that repression causes anxiety. If this hypothesis were correct, Freud could relieve Hans' phobia by removing his repression. And the very procedure that might help his patient—which was Freud's first responsibility—would at the same time be an experiment to test his hypothesis. That is, if bringing Hans' repressed feelings back into consciousness did result in disappearance of the phobia, the hypothesis would be supported.
Freud proceeded to try this with Hans:

I then disclosed to him that he was afraid of his father, precisely because he was so fond of his mother. It must be, I told him, that he thought his father was angry with him on that account; but this was not so, his father was fond of him in spite of it, and he might admit everything to him without any fear.[9]

On several occasions shortly afterward, Hans butted his head against his father, bit him, and "defied" him in various childish ways, apparently indicating that Freud had been at least partly successful in removing the repression.
And what was the effect of this treatment upon Hans' anxiety? His father reported that the next day Hans seemed somewhat less anxious and stood before the front door of their apartment building for an entire hour. Sometimes he ran inside when he saw a horse and cart approaching, but then he would change his mind and return. In short, his anxiety seemed somewhat decreased. It did not disappear, however, until several months later.
The immediate outcome of this little experiment neither clearly supported nor clearly disproved Freud's hypothesis. Although it began to look as if the hypothesis might be false, it could still be argued that Hans remained somewhat anxious only because the removal of his repressions was not yet complete.
Years later, however, Freud decided that the removal of repression had failed to decrease patients' anxiety too often for his early theory to be correct.[10] He looked for a new hypothesis which would fit both the

[8] Freud, *Collected Papers,* III, 194; and Strachey, *Standard Edition,* X, 51.
[9] Freud, *Collected Papers,* III, 184–85; and Strachey, *Standard Edition,* X, 42.
[10] Sigmund Freud, *The Problem of Anxiety* (New York: W. W. Norton & Company, Inc., 1936).

observation that anxiety and repression are related, and the observation that removal of repression often does not remove anxiety. He then adopted the hypothesis that anxiety causes repression. The new view was that the individual bedeviled by anxiety unconsciously defends himself from anxiety-provoking thoughts by repressing or mentally avoiding them,[11] somewhat as one would physically avoid dangerous objects in his physical environment.

This new theory has been widely accepted. But, partly because this theory does not explain everything about avoidance, psychologists have continued to do research on this topic. Some of the more recent research will be described in later chapters.

[11] "Repression" and "mental avoidance" will be treated as synonyms throughout this book. Strictly speaking, however, psychoanalysis has distinguished at least two kinds of mental avoidance—repression and denial. Whereas *repression* is a complete blocking out of internal factors such as forbidden impulses, and of events associated with them, *denial* is a blocking out of external factors such as environmental barriers to the satisfaction of one's impulses.

3 Evaluation of Freud's Study of Little Hans

Freud's study of Little Hans is an example of both a case study and an exploratory study. A case study is a detailed study of one individual or group, and an exploratory study is a search for new hypotheses. The primary reason the clinician makes a detailed study of a particular individual is, of course, that he is trying to cure that individual. A common side benefit of the case study, however, is a set of new hypotheses about how the mind works in people in general.

Most exploratory studies, including the present one, have these characteristics:

1. They suggest new questions and hypotheses.
2. Their evidence for accuracy of measurement is weak.
3. Their evidence for generalizability is weak.
4. Their evidence for causality is weak.

It should be made clear that my evaluation of the Little Hans case is not necessarily that of all psychologists or psychiatrists. Psychoanalysts, in particular, are likely to be less critical than I am of the evidence for measurement accuracy, generalizability, and causality provided by this study.

THE IDENTIFICATION OF NEW QUESTIONS

An invaluable contribution of the Little Hans study, and of much of Freud's work, was the identification of important new questions—for example, the question of exactly how anxiety is related to conflict and repression. This question seems important because it may provide a key to the understanding and conquest of neurotic fear.

What are some of the characteristics of a study like this which make it a fertile source of hypotheses? The main thing to notice is that Freud and Hans' father did not choose one topic—such as Hans' affection for his mother—and concentrate doggedly upon it. Instead, they moved from topic to topic as their own hunches and Hans' comments led them. (The variety of the topics touched upon in this study is much more striking in Freud's own report than it is in the selective summary presented in Chapter 2.) Of course such exploration is not restricted to the case study. Other sources of information which may suggest new hypotheses to the observant researcher are his own experience, libraries, and experts.

Although broad exploration is the best way to produce new hypotheses, it usually cannot provide adequate evidence for them. That task usually must be left to later studies which concentrate upon particular hypotheses suggested by the exploratory study. This sequence of broad exploration followed by narrow, focused inspection is useful not only in psychology and other sciences, but in all kinds of observation. For example, if you had a chance to tour Europe for twenty days, would you choose to visit twenty localities for one day each, or one locality for twenty days? Many tourists would prefer to get a broader though more superficial view of Europe on their first trip and then, on later trips, to concentrate on places they had found particularly interesting before.

While the need for breadth of observation is probably greatest when a particular area is first studied, it continues to exist even later on. Even researchers taking a more focused approach often use any extra "room" in their studies for exploratory purposes. The kinds of unexpected findings that can appear when researchers keep their eyes open are illustrated in Pavlov's studies described in Chapter 8, and in Solomon's study reported in Chapter 10.

ACCURACY OF MEASUREMENT

The very breadth and flexibility which made Freud's study of Hans such a fertile source of new hypotheses prevented it from gathering adequate evidence for accuracy of measurement, or for generalizability and causality.

Reliability. Although the effects of observer bias were not ascertained in this study, we can make some guesses about them. Ordinarily, hard-to-define variables like anxiety, repression, and conflict are difficult to measure in an unbiased way unless special pains are taken to specify exactly what the observer is to do, leaving no room for his own judgment. Since this was not done in Freud's study, it is quite possible that the father's biases—including his expectations about what Hans would do and say—influenced his observations. One point at which this seems to have happened is when he asked Hans, "When the horse fell down, did you think of your daddy?" Clearly this was a leading question—that is, one phrased so as to lead Hans to give the expected affirmative answer. Thus the answer that was given—"Perhaps. Yes. It's possible"—might well have reflected the father's expectations more than Hans' actual reactions to the fallen horse.

Another factor undoubtedly left uncontrolled in this study—as well as in many other clinical case studies—is the phrasing of questions. Whether a clinician asks "Are you still feeling anxious today?" or "Is your anxiety less today?" might well influence a patient's answer. One way to solve this problem would be always to use the same words to ask about a given topic. However, many therapists would object that the use of standard questions would destroy the informal, spontaneous atmosphere they are trying to create.

Validity. There are no noticeable errors specific to the validity of these observations, but it should be pointed out that unreliability implies invalidity. Insofar as observations are influenced by such extraneous factors as observer bias and the phrasing of questions, they are not being determined by the variable they are intended to measure and are therefore invalid.

If the observations of Hans were of questionable accuracy, this renders useless any evidence for generalizability or causality. After all, if a set of observations does not validly measure variables X and Y, it is senseless to try to find out from those observations whether X causes Y, and then to generalize any relationships discovered between them. Nevertheless, since our main interest is in methods per se, we will go on to discuss the evidence in this study for causality and generalizability.

GENERALIZABILITY

When Freud thought he had found that anxiety caused repression in his neurotic patients, he generalized that principle to all humanity. Was this justified? On the one hand, it seems quite possible that neurotics are distinctly different from normal individuals. On the other hand, Freud argued that the line between normality and abnormality is often a vague one. For example, he guessed that the phobia was noticed in Hans, not because his problems were particularly severe, but merely because his parents were unusually observant. Though plausible arguments can be made on both sides of this question, the only conclusive solution would be to gather evidence about the psychological problems of normal individuals and to see how they compared with those of neurotics. One study of the mental health of normal adults is described in Chapter 6.

CAUSALITY

Freud thought he had removed, at least to some extent, Hans' repressions. If so, this study could be considered an experiment testing the hypothesis that repression causes anxiety or, more accurately, that removal of repression causes a decrease in anxiety. However, it was a poorly controlled experiment, as will be shown.

Relationships. There were in effect two conditions in Freud's experiment —the repressed and the unrepressed—and Hans was at first in the one and then in the other. Since the amount of anxiety Hans showed in the two conditions differed somewhat, repression and anxiety appeared to be related.

Control. Were anxiety and repression the only variables that differed in the two conditions, or were some influential extraneous factors also allowed to vary? Certainly many extraneous variables were controlled. For example, since Hans was used as his own control, all of his stable characteristics, such as intelligence, were controlled.

However, using the subject as his own control always raises the problem of controlling time. That is, if one subject is in two conditions, he must be in one earlier and in the other later. Hans' decline in anxiety—in addition to being related to the removal of repression—was also related to the passage of time. Thus it is possible that time alone was responsible for Hans' recovery and that the removal of his repressions had nothing at all to do with it. This is a possibility that cannot be taken lightly; after all, many patients in mental hospitals have recovered without any therapy whatsoever.

The standard way of bringing the time variable under control would be to compare the progress of Hans, who had both time and treatment in his favor, with the progress of a similar neurotic who had no treatment, but only time to help him. Only if Hans improved more than the untreated patient would it be concluded that the treatment had helped to decrease anxiety.

You may be thinking that it would be difficult to find neurotic persons willing to postpone treatment for the sake of such an experiment. This is, indeed, a serious difficulty; nevertheless, some studies of this type have been attempted.

Order. Since the independent variable was manipulated in Freud's experiment, we can be fairly confident that the removal of repression occurred before any change in anxiety. However, this is not particularly helpful to know because, due to lack of control, it is quite possible that there was no direct causal relationship between repression and anxiety.

A WORD IN DEFENSE OF FREUD'S METHODS

Because Freud's case studies did not provide very adequate evidence regarding his theories, nonpsychoanalysts have frequently concluded that these theories should be tested by methods that can provide more adequate evidence.

Perhaps this is a good suggestion for some Freudian hypotheses and a poor suggestion for others. If it is hypotheses about neurosis itself that one wishes to test, possibly the psychoanalytic case study, or something like it, is the only method that can be used. Whatever its research inadequacies, Freud's method of interviewing patients who, during their long association with him, had learned to trust him even with their most shameful secrets might possibly be the only effective way to study neurosis. On the other hand, if one wishes to test hypotheses which, although perhaps derived from Freud's work with neurotics, concern something less private, there seems to be no reason why he cannot use methods other than the case study. It is this kind of derived hypothesis which is tested in some of the laboratory experiments described in later chapters.

4 Thurstone and Willoughby Measure Neuroticism

Was Freud really measuring anxiety? Unfortunately, he did not gather all the evidence needed to answer this question. In fact, most of the techniques for gathering such evidence had not yet been discovered at the time of Hans' phobia. In this chapter the major techniques of gathering evidence about accuracy of measurement are illustrated in the account of two psychologists, Thurstone and Willoughby, who developed measures of "neuroticism." Willoughby's measure, which was based on Thurstone's, is particularly relevant here because it has been used by psychiatrist Joseph Wolpe, whose work is described in Chapter 12.

THE THURSTONE PERSONALITY SCHEDULE[1]

Louis L. Thurstone was a practical man. His first publication, written at the age of 18, was a letter to *Scientific American* suggesting how the diversion of water from Niagara Falls to hydroelectric plants could be prevented from ruining the beauty of the falls. In college he studied engineering and developed a new type of motion picture camera in which Thomas Edison was interested.

When he took up the study of psychology in graduate school, the new field seemed to him to be sadly lacking in solid knowledge. Nevertheless,

[1] The material in this section is based largely on L. L. and Thelma Thurstone, "A Neurotic Inventory," *Journal of Social Psychology*, I (1930), 3–30.

he did find a few areas in psychology which suited his tastes, since they seemed ready for solid, scientific development. The area to which he probably contributed most throughout his career was that of psychological measurement.

In the 1920's, while Thurstone was a professor at the University of Chicago, he and his wife saw a need for a test that would identify students who had neurotic tendencies, so that they could be offered help by the university counseling service. One characteristic that is desirable in a measuring instrument is that it require little time to administer and score. The Thurstones decided to use the kind of psychological test that probably best achieves this goal—the *inventory*, printed multiple-choice questions asking people about themselves.

Their first step was to collect as many neuroticism questions as possible from existing inventories. They found over 600 such questions, which had originally come from textbook descriptions of neurotic symptoms, from hospital files on neurotic patients, and from other sources. After duplicates were omitted, 223 questions remained, in which the subject was asked whether he felt and did a wide variety of things. While some questions were clearly about anxiety, others concerned sleepwalking, impulsiveness, and many other topics. Because this inventory is still used today, none of the questions can be quoted here. The following, however, is an example of the kind of question the Thurstones used:

Yes No ?   Do you often feel anxious about things?

The person taking the test was to describe himself by circling yes, no, or, if neither of those answers seemed applicable, the question mark.

The hope was that the number of neurotic symptoms a subject reported would, if his answers were accurate, indicate how strong his neurotic tendencies were. But how accurately would subjects answer such questions? Possibly some subjects would realize that they were often anxious, yet circle "no" for the above question because they did not want to admit it. The Thurstones tried to encourage their subjects— University of Chicago freshmen—to answer truthfully by including in the instructions an assurance that answers would not affect grades, a pledge that answers to individual questions would be kept confidential (although each student's total score would be sent to his dean), and the following statement:

It has been found that some of the brightest students have emotional and personality difficulties which can be overcome with suitable counsel if the difficulties are known. It will therefore be to your own advantage to answer the questions as truthfully as possible.[2]

2 Thurstone, "A Neurotic Inventory," p. 4.

In other words, they were telling the student that he need not be afraid to admit neurotic symptoms, because such an admission could only help him.

The instructions and questions were given to almost 700 subjects. From the completed questionnaires was derived information about the neuroticism of the individual students and information about the adequacy of the measuring instrument itself.

The student scores were presumably put to good use by the University of Chicago counseling service, and were analyzed by the Thurstones for their relationships with other variables. The Thurstones found that women received a higher mean neuroticism score than men (43.8 versus 37.3), fraternity and sorority members received a slightly lower mean than independents, and students receiving high scores tended to have higher grades (although no higher intelligence) than those receiving low scores. These results are mentioned only so that you may puzzle over them if you wish.

VALIDILITY OF THE THURSTONE INVENTORY

Also of great interest to the Thurstones was the information that could be derived from the completed questionnaires concerning characteristics of the inventory itself. The analysis they used is relevant to both reliability and validity, but only the latter will be discussed here. A more complete discussion of the type of analysis they used can be found in Chapter 5.

The main assumption upon which their analysis was based was that the total test was a valid measure of neuroticism, even though some individual test items might not have been. If this were true, one could find out how valid each item was by finding out how strongly scores on that item were related to total test scores. Unlike the usual case, this kind of relationship indicates that both variables are measuring the same thing, not that one is causing the other.

To calculate the item-test relationships, the Thurstones first added up each student's total neuroticism score, giving one point for each question answered in what they assumed to be the more "neurotic" way. They then took the 50 questionnaires with the highest total scores and the 50 with the lowest total scores. For every question, they looked to see how many of the 50 high scorers had given the more "neurotic" answer, and how many of the 50 low scorers had given it. They found that for every single question, more high scorers than low had given this answer. Thus every question, at least to some extent, was measuring the same thing the test as a whole measured, presumably neuroticism.

One possible weak point in this analysis is the crucial assumption that total scores reflected primarily neuroticism. To check the truth of this assumption, one could find another measure of neuroticism—for example, clinical diagnosis—and use it as a *criterion,* or standard against which to compare the Thurstone inventory. That is, one could find out whether persons diagnosed as neurotic obtained higher Thurstone scores than did normal persons. Such a study has in fact been done.

F. L. Schotte, a psychologist then employed at the Henry Ford Hospital in Detroit, obtained scores on the Thurstone Personality Schedule from several categories of persons connected with the hospital. The categories and their median[3] Thurstone scores are indicated in Table 1.

TABLE 1   SCORES OF VARIOUS GROUPS ON THE
THURSTONE PERSONALITY SCHEDULE*

Group	Median score	No. of subjects
Normal persons at Ford Hospital (e.g., doctors and nurses)	35	200
Thurstone freshmen	34	682
Mental patients (mainly neurotic) at Ford Hospital	64	275 (182 neurotic)
Applicants for professional positions at Ford Hospital	20	130

* After E. L. Schotte, "Personality Tests in Clinical Practice," *Journal of Abnormal and Social Psychology,* XXXII (1937), 236–39. Copyright 1937 by the American Psychological Association. Used by permission.

One thing to notice about Schotte's results is that the normal subjects did report some neurotic symptoms. Apparently it is normal to have a certain number of neurotic symptoms.

A greater median number of symptoms, however, was reported by the mental patients, about two-thirds of whom had been diagnosed as neurotic. This is evidence that the Thurstone inventory is, at least to some extent, a valid measure of neuroticism.

Another finding was that Schotte's normal group obtained almost exactly the same median score as did the Thurstones' University of Chicago freshmen. The fact that these two normal groups obtained similar neuroticism scores further strengthens our confidence in the accuracy of the Thurstone inventory.

Finally, the fact that applicants for jobs at Ford Hospital obtained a median score of only 20, 15 points lower than the median for the doctors

[3] A median is that score which half the subjects in a group surpass and half fall below.

and nurses there, seems to support the Thurstones' suspicion that if a person is motivated to make himself look non-neurotic on this inventory (as job applicants presumably are), he will have little trouble in doing so.

WILLOUGHBY'S MODIFICATION OF THE THURSTONE INVENTORY [4]

Ever since he was psychoanalyzed during his graduate school years, Raymond R. Willoughby was primarily interested in the clinical area of psychology. After receiving his Ph.D., he joined the faculty at Clark University in Worcester, Massachusetts, and carried on a small psychotherapeutic practice on the side. When the Thurstones published their neurotic inventory, Willoughby saw the potential usefulness of this kind of measure, but he thought the Thurstone inventory too long and time-consuming for many purposes. He therefore selected what he considered the 25 best Thurstone items to make up a shorter scale. Willoughby chose his items on several bases. For one thing, he chose items which the Thurstones had found to relate particularly strongly to total test scores. Hence his items (and therefore his test) are probably highly valid.

So far Willoughby's neurotic inventory had the following advantages:

1. It could be administered to many individuals at once.
2. It took only a few minutes to fill out.
3. It could be quickly scored.
4. It was probably at least reasonably valid.

Now evidence had to be shown for the instrument's reliability. There are several distinct kinds of reliability, all involving the consistency of the scores obtained by comparable subjects on comparable tests.

One kind of reliability that Willoughby checked on is internal consistency. This he estimated by the split-half method, which involved administering his test to a group of subjects, then splitting the test in two and calculating for each subject one score for the first 12 items and another for the last 12. (The middle item apparently was omitted from this analysis.) The two halves being considered as two comparable tests, internal consistency was indicated by the strength of the relationship between scores for those halves. Suffice it to say that for several groups of students this relationship was very strong indeed, indicating high internal consistency.

[4] The material in this section is based largely on R. R. Willoughby, "Some Properties of the Thurstone Personality Schedule and a Suggested Revision," *Journal of Social Psychology*, III (1932), 401–24; and on R. R. Willoughby, "Norms for the Clark-Thurstone Inventory," *Journal of Social Psychology*, V (1934), 91–97.

Another kind of reliability—stability over time—was estimated by the test-retest method.   This involves giving the same subjects exactly the same test at two different times.   Willoughby gave his inventory to 36 University of California students and then, about two and a half months later, gave it to the same students again.   Correlating the two sets of scores, Willoughby obtained a coefficient of 0.89, high enough to indicate quite satisfactory stability over time.   An explanation of correlation coefficients can be found in Chapter 5.

Thus Willoughby's shortened inventory proved to have both high internal consistency and high stability over time.   Adding these two kinds of reliability to the already known attributes of this inventory just about completes its credentials.   Although more information can always be gathered about the reliability and validity of a measuring instrument, the Willoughby inventory has already been shown to meet reasonable standards of adequacy.

It may seem that it takes a lot of work to develop an adequate measuring instrument.   Often this is true.   Once developed, however, an instrument can be used by other psychologists.   One who has regularly used the Willoughby inventory is Joseph Wolpe, a psychiatrist whose work is described in Chapter 12.

5 Evaluation of Willoughby's Neurotic Inventory

Psychological measurement can be defined as the assigning of numbers or labels (such as "male" or "female") to subjects according to rules. A major goal of the Thurstones and Willoughby was to develop rules for measuring neuroticism accurately. This goal seems an important one because accurate research on neuroticism is badly needed, and it would be impossible without an accurate measuring instrument.

How successful was Willoughby in attaining this goal? Probably quite successful, because he used effective methods of test development. This chapter describes some standard methods, many of them used by Willoughby, of (1) minimizing measurement error, and (2) estimating two aspects of the resulting accuracy of measurement—reliability and validity.

MINIMIZING ERROR OF MEASUREMENT

Willoughby wanted scores on his inventory to be caused primarily by subjects' neuroticism. Unless he did something to prevent it, however, those scores might be affected by extraneous variables: stimulus variables such as what instructions were given and what specific questions were asked; subject variables such as boredom or the tendency to make socially desirable responses; and the biases of those who were observing the subjects' responses and scoring them. The way to keep such extraneous variables from distorting scores is to prevent differences from occurring on them. Two ways of doing this are standardizing the test and increasing the number of items in it.

Willoughby standardized his test by specifying what instructions were to be used, what questions were to be asked, and what procedure was to be used to score answers. This had the effect of holding all these variables constant from one administration of the test to another.

Other variables were probably controlled by randomization. Each subject, for example, might have misread a few questions in a random way. If so, some misreadings might have inflated his neuroticism score, others might have deflated it, thus balancing the score. As previously mentioned, this balancing process provides better control when more separate measurements enter into the total score. This means that the more items there are in the test, the more accurate is the total test score, other factors being equal. Despite this advantage of long tests, however, Willoughby chose to use relatively few of the Thurstones' items, apparently feeling that the gain in brevity would be worth the loss in accuracy.

Although the methods just described are likely to increase the accuracy of a measuring instrument, there is no way of knowing just how much accuracy has been achieved without checking on it. Some standard methods of checking on reliability and validity are described next.

ESTIMATING RELIABILITY

One method Willoughby used to estimate the accuracy of his test was to administer it twice to the same subjects. Each of these subjects' neuroticism, as well as his other stable characteristics, should have remained approximately the same from one administration to the other. Therefore, to the extent that the inventory was accurately measuring neuroticism or some other stable characteristic, each subject's scores should have been similar, consistent, or reliable on the two administrations.

On the other hand, in working with a relatively unstable variable, such as mood, we would want the scores to change considerably from one time to another. The general rule is this: whatever a variable does, an accurate measure of that variable will do the same.

The importance reliability can have is illustrated in the following extreme example. Suppose a clinical psychologist uses a particular test of anxiety to help him decide whether a patient should be referred to a mental hospital. Partly on the basis of the patient's high score on this test, the decision is to refer him. When the patient arrives at the mental hospital a few days later, he is given, as part of the standard admissions procedure, a series of tests which includes the one given to him earlier by the clinical psychologist. This time the patient's anxiety score is not nearly high enough to justify his referral to the hospital.

One possible explanation is of course that the patient has actually become less anxious in the past few days. However, it seems unlikely that the neurotic kind of anxiety the test is supposed to measure would change drastically in so short a time. Therefore the psychologist, when he learned of this, would undoubtedly be dismayed and—particularly if the same test had produced inconsistent scores for other patients—would quite possibly discard the test, concluding that it was not reliable enough for his purposes. To avoid this kind of embarrassment, one should, before using a particular test, demand evidence that it has the kind and degree of reliability one needs.

Relationships and correlation coefficients. Before there is any further discussion of test reliability, it is necessary to understand the terms "relationship" and "correlation coefficient." Two variables are said to be related when differences on one coincide with differences on the other. Table 2 shows a hypothetical relationship between answers to the question "Do you prefer the Republican or the Democratic Party?" asked first in January, and asked again of the same subjects in March. These two variables are related because the same people who differed politically in January also tended to differ politically in March. That is, of the January Republicans, most (85 per cent) were still Republicans in March. And of the January Democrats, most (90 per cent) were still Democrats. This particular relationship, by the way, shows this measuring device to have considerable—but not perfect—reliability of one kind.

TABLE 2   HYPOTHETICAL RELATIONSHIP BETWEEN TWO REPORTS OF PARTY PREFERENCE BY THE SAME SUBJECTS

| | | January | |
		Republican	Democratic
March	Democratic	15%	90%
	Republican	85%	10%
		100%	100%

A slightly different form of relationship is illustrated in Table 3, which shows hypothetical data on subjects' mean anxiety and their annual income.

TABLE 3 HYPOTHETICAL RELATIONSHIP BETWEEN
ANXIETY AND ANNUAL INCOME

	Annual income	
	Below $8,000	$8,000 and up
Mean anxiety	3.8	21.4

A third form of relationship is illustrated in the tables in Figure 1. A linear relationship (the kind psychologists have been most interested in) is present in those tables where height tends to increase (or decrease) by equal steps as self-confidence increases by equal steps.

The tables in Figure 1 are arranged so as to make clear the fact that relationships can vary in two respects: *direction* and *strength*. Tables 1 and 3 show relationships that are positive in direction, that is, where higher scores on one variable tend to go with higher scores on the other. Tables 2 and 4 show negative relationships; there, higher scores on one variable tend to go with lower scores on the other. Although there are always two directions a relationship may take, it is sometimes not possible to call one positive and the other negative, such as when the relationship involves a variable like "Republican-Democrat," where neither classification can be considered higher than the other.

Strength of relationship is quite different from direction. The positive and negative relationships in tables 1 and 2 are both very strong—a large mean change occurs in one variable when the other changes. The positive and negative relationships in tables 3 and 4 are both of moderate strength. That is, only a moderate mean change occurs in one variable when the other changes. Finally, table 5 shows no relationship whatsoever—in it, neither variable changes at all when the other changes.

Although adjectives like "strong" and "moderate" have some value in describing relationships, they are very inexact. Fortunately, there is available a more exact descriptive tool—the correlation coefficient, symbolized r. The method for computing a correlation coefficient from two sets of scores cannot be explained here, but something can be said about how to interpret it. A correlation coefficient can be divided into a numerical part, and a plus or minus sign which precedes it. The size of the numerical part indicates the strength of the relationship; r's of 1.00 (i.e., +1.00) and −1.00 indicate the strongest possible relationships, while an r of 0.00 indicates no relationship at all. The plus or minus sign indicates the direction of the relationship; for example, 0.73 indicates a positive relationship, while −0.73 indicates a relationship of exactly the same strength, but negative in direction. The correlation coefficients cor-

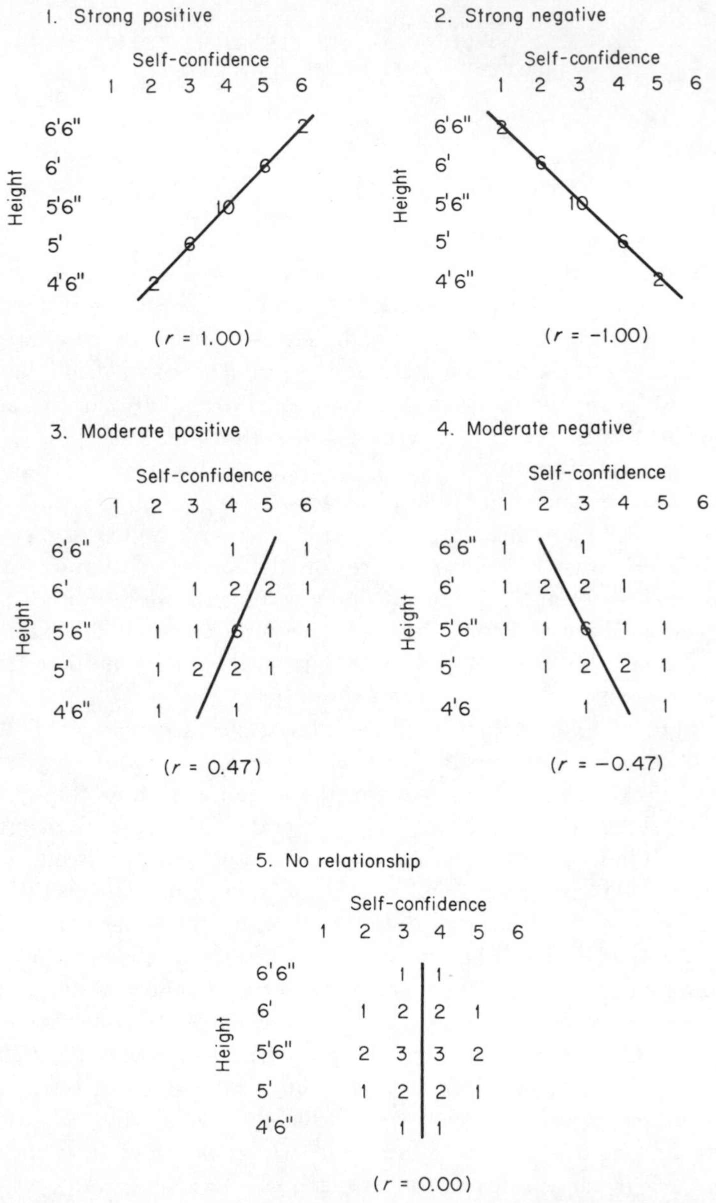

FIGURE 1 Hypothetical relationships between height (to nearest half foot) and a measure of self-confidence in men. The numbers in the tables are numbers of subjects obtaining each combination of self-confidence and height scores. The line drawn through each table passes through the mean self-confidence for each height. Other things equal, the more these means change from height to height, the stronger the relationship in the table.

responding to the relationships in Figure 1 are indicated there in parentheses.

Types of test reliability. All the major types of test reliability are estimated by computing coefficients of correlation between scores obtained by comparable subjects on two comparable tests. Briefly, these types are as follows:

1. *Objectivity,* which is estimated by correlating the scores given the same subjects by two different observers. This kind of reliability is necessarily high when a scoring procedure is completely "cut and dried," as it is for the Willoughby inventory, and in such cases no one would go to the trouble of using two scorers. However, in studies where the observer has to make great use of his own judgment—as when he is asked to watch subjects' behavior and rate them on activity, efficiency, leadership, or some other such characteristics—it is standard procedure to check on objectivity.

2. *Equivalence of forms,* which is estimated by correlating subjects' scores on two forms of a test. The forms, although containing different items, have been made essentially equivalent.

3. *Internal consistency,* which is estimated by correlating subjects' scores on different parts of the same test. One way of dividing a test into parts for this purpose is the split-half method, used by Willoughby. The correlation coefficients of internal consistency that Willoughby obtained were in the 0.80's and 0.90's.

   Naturally, it is only when most of the items in a test are meant to measure the same variable that it makes sense to consider different parts of that test as comparable measuring devices, and thus to expect them to correlate highly.

4. *Stability over time,* which is estimated by correlating the scores subjects obtain on exactly the same test given to them at two different times. This is the type of reliability for which Willoughby found a correlation of 0.89, and that seemed to be lacking in the anxiety measure used by the hypothetical clinical psychologist who referred a patient to a mental hospital.

Statistical reliability. We will not meet a study in which statistical reliability is an important concern until the next chapter. However, the topic is introduced at this point so that the contrast between this type of reliability and test reliability can be made as sharply as possible.

Whereas test reliability concerns the consistency of test scores, statistical reliability deals with the consistency of a statistic. (A statistic is a number, such as a mean, which summarizes a group of scores.) High reliability in a test does not guarantee high reliability in statistics based on that test, and vice versa.

Suppose that a researcher uses the Willoughby scale on two groups of subjects which initially had equally high neuroticism, but which have in the meantime been treated with two different therapies. Group A now obtains a mean Willoughby score of 20, and group B, a mean of 32. The statistic of interest here is the mean difference—or difference between the two means—of 12. Therapy A seems to lower anxiety 12 points more than does B, but is this statistic reliable? That is, if the study were repeated on two other, comparable groups, would a similar mean difference occur?

As we have already seen, test reliability is estimated in the straightforward way of measuring subjects twice and using the correlation coefficient to determine how consistent the two sets of scores are. In contrast, the estimation of statistical reliability requires only that subjects be measured once. These scores are then "plugged into" mathematical formulas which estimate the degree of reliability that can be expected of given summary statistics. One component of these formulas is the number of subjects used in the study; the more subjects used, the more similar the results would probably be if the study were repeated.

The researcher is often interested in knowing not only how reliable his statistical results are, but also how certain he can be that the "true" result is different from zero. In the above example, the obtained mean difference was 12 points; is it possible that this difference is completely due to random error, and that in reality there is no difference in the effects of the two treatments? Suffice it to say that the larger the obtained difference and the greater its reliability, the less likely it is to be completely due to random error. When the estimated probability that such a result is entirely due to random error is found to be .05 (1/20) or less, it is standard practice for psychologists to consider the result at least partly real, or "significantly different from zero."

ESTIMATING VALIDITY

The fact that the Willoughby inventory proved to be high in several types of test reliability shows only that it is measuring some stable subject variable—perhaps anxiety, but perhaps not. To name only one other possibility, it could be measuring a tendency to make socially desirable responses. This particular possibility exists for the Willoughby and most other inventories because the subject can easily see what kinds of answers will make him look better (less neurotic, in the case of the Willoughby) than others.

Is the test measuring what it is supposed to measure? One way to estimate validity is to compare subjects' scores on the test being validated with their scores on another, unquestionably valid (criterion) measure of the same variable. The new test, if it turns out to be highly related to the criterion measure, must itself be highly valid.

The importance validity can have may be seen by returning to the hypothetical clinical psychologist mentioned earlier. Suppose that by now he has replaced his former anxiety test with a new one of proven reliability. Once again he refers a patient to the mental hospital, this time partly because of a high score on the new test. When this patient goes through the hospital's testing program, he obtains a high anxiety score on the same test the clinical psychologist gave him—demonstrating the reliability of that instrument—but makes a low score on another, more highly regarded, measure of anxiety. Needless to say, the psychologist will not be overjoyed about this, either. It raises the possibility that what his newly adopted test is reliably measuring is something other than anxiety.

Briefly, the types of validity are:

1. *Content validity,* which is estimated by determining how adequately the questions in a course exam, for example, cover the content of that course. For another example, the Manifest Anxiety Scale[1] was created by asking clinical psychologists to select, from a large number of items, those which measured surface anxiety. The resulting test has content validity because experts judged that its items have the desired content. This is quite different from the next two types of validity because content validation does *not* involve the use of a criterion measure.

2. *Concurrent validity,* which is estimated by relating the measure being validated to a criterion measure administered to the same subjects at substantially the same time. One of the most common ways of doing this is to find two or more groups known to differ on the criterion (for example, productive versus unproductive managers; creative versus uncreative architects), then to give the new test to these groups to see if they get different mean scores. A question often raised about such studies is whether the criterion measure is adequate; it must have proven itself to be valid if it is to be a useful criterion measure.

3. *Predictive validity,* which is estimated by correlating the new measure with a criterion measure that is administered to the same subjects at some later time. This kind of validity would be essential for a test used to predict how successful a particular therapy will be with various kinds of patients. In this example, the predictor test would be given to patients at the beginning of therapy, and the criterion would be a measure of how much improvement the same patients showed at the end of therapy.

4. *Construct validity,* which is estimated by (a) hypothesizing how anxiety, for example, relates to certain other variables and then (b) finding out if scores on the "anxiety" scale being validated are related to them in the same way. For instance, one might hypothesize that anxiety is higher before a person takes an exam than after, and higher during a horror movie than during a comedy. The "anxiety" test would then be given to subjects in those situa-

[1] Janet A. Taylor, "A Personality Scale of Manifest Anxiety," *Journal of Abnormal and Social Psychology,* IIL (1953), 285–90.

tions to see if the scores varied as anxiety was expected to vary. If so, the test might be measuring anxiety.

Many studies of this sort are usually needed to produce much confidence in the validity of a measure. In contrast, it takes only one study to correlate a test with a criterion. For this reason, construct validation methods are not ordinarily used when an adequate criterion measure is available.

SELECTING ITEMS THAT CORRELATE HIGHLY
WITH A TEST

It is a frequent practice to correlate subjects' scores on each item of a test with their total test scores, as the Thurstones did, and then to select those items that had the highest correlation with the test to make up an improved instrument, as Willoughby did. This practice can affect both validity and reliability.

Suppose that a researcher sets out to collect a number of test items which measure anxiety. Although he might make a few mistakes, probably he will choose successfully in the case of most items. If so, the total scores on his test will reflect primarily anxiety. Individual items that correlate highly with total scores probably also reflect primarily anxiety, and low correlated items probably measure primarily some other variable.

What, then, will be the effects of discarding items having low correlations with such a test? First, this will increase the test's reliability of the internal consistency sort, since weeding out nonanxiety items will leave only items measuring anxiety. In the second place, since anxiety is the one variable this test is supposed to measure, the new purified test will also be more valid than the old one.

GENERALIZABILITY

Strictly speaking, demonstrating that a measuring instrument is reliable and valid for a particular kind of subject and stimulus situation does not guarantee that the instrument is also accurate for other kinds.

One case where we would have particularly good reason to doubt the accuracy of the Thurstone and Willoughby tests is where they were applied to persons highly motivated to look good, such as job applicants. Even this reasoning, however, could be wrong. The only way to find out for certain how accurate a test is for the job applicant or for any other kind of subject is to carry out reliability and validity studies on that kind of subject.

6

Gurin Surveys the Mental Health of the Average U.S. Adult[1]

Have you ever had Oedipal feelings toward your parents? If you think not, Freud would disagree with you. He thought his theories applied to everyone, not just to the small group of nineteenth-century Viennese neurotics he studied. While Freud may have been right, his evidence was certainly not sufficient to support such generalization. The kind of evidence required for generalization is illustrated in this chapter in a study on the mental health of the average U.S. adult.

According to the limited information available on the subject in 1955, the national mental health picture was black. It appeared that the problem was a large one: experts estimated that as many as six out of every hundred Americans suffered "serious" mental disorders. The problem also appeared costly: for example, veterans' mental illness was costing the federal government nearly $600 million annually. Most discouraging of all, the methods of treatment being used appeared to be ineffective: for example, patients in their second year in a mental hospital faced estimated odds of sixteen to one against ever being released.[2]

In the face of estimates like these, the 1955 Congress appropriated one

[1] The material in this chapter is based largely on G. Gurin, J. Veroff, and Sheila Feld, *Americans View Their Mental Health; A Nationwide Interview Survey* (New York: Basic Books, Inc., Publishers, 1960).

[2] *The New York Times*, March 9, 1955, p. 22, col. 6, and March 27, 1955, p. 64, cols. 1–4.

and a quarter million dollars for a series of studies to gather more information on American mental health. These studies were intended to lay the basis for plans to improve the situation.

Soon afterward, a number of national foundations and associations interested in mental health formed the Joint Commission on Mental Health to oversee the studies envisioned by Congress. Under the auspices of the Commission, studies were done on the costs of mental illness, on the training and availability of mental health personnel, and on other related topics. While most of these studies focused primarily upon the mental patient, the Commission also felt it important to find out something about the average adult citizen. How great were his psychological problems, and how did he react to them?

How was the Commission to get the information it wanted? Although it certainly would have been convenient to use previous findings on other groups, it would probably not be wise to assume that what was true of them would also be true of the average U.S. adult. For example, the theories that Freud developed from his patients might not apply to the average modern-day American because the two groups differ in their nationality and their era.

It appeared, then, that a new study should be carried out—this one on the average U.S. adult himself. In 1957 the Commission hired the University of Michigan Survey Research Center to conduct a nationwide survey on the mental health of the normal U.S. adult. The Survey Research Center is a nonprofit organization which maintains the special facilities and skilled staff needed to conduct large surveys. Dr. Gerald Gurin and his colleagues, Drs. Joseph Veroff and Sheila Feld—all employees of the Survey Research Center—were placed in charge of translating the Joint Commission's questions into a survey which would effectively answer them. To do this, they had to (1) find "the average U.S. adult" and (2) obtain from him accurate information about his mental health.

FINDING "THE AVERAGE U.S. ADULT"

The Joint Commission wanted results that were representative of the U.S. adult population. That is, if exactly 42 per cent of all U.S. adults could correctly define "neurosis," then the percentage of those surveyed who could correctly define it should be close to 42.

Gurin attempted to ensure the representativeness of his results by using largely random methods to draw his sample of subjects from the adult American population. You will recall that a random sample tends to be, on the average, equivalent in every respect to the population from which it was drawn.

To begin with, a sample of about 2825 adults was selected. (The method used for the selection will be described in the next chapter.) When interviewers knocked at their doors, however, about 225 (8 per cent) refused to be interviewed, and about 140 (5 per cent) could not be found at home, even after from three to ten attempts. The sample was thus shrunk somewhat by nonrandom factors and therefore was probably not as representative as it had been on the drawing board; however, this percentage of sample loss is usual in surveys of this kind.

Now that a group of persons representing fairly closely the average U.S. adult had agreed to be interviewed, how could the interviewers find out what they really thought about their mental health?

SURVEYING THE MENTAL HEALTH OF THE SAMPLED SUBJECTS

Since the topic of mental illness is usually considered a sensitive one, Gurin expected that subjects might show some reluctance to answer the interviewers' questions. In fact, however, no such reluctance appeared. The reason for this probably lies partly in "human nature" and partly in effective planning by the investigators.

It is often not realized that people are usually willing to talk freely about even the most sensitive topics to an impartial stranger. For example, there recently appeared at my door an interviewer collecting opinions about political candidates. Probably like most people, I was quite willing to cooperate. After all, it isn't often that one gets a chance to tell about himself and his opinions to someone who listens carefully and never contradicts.

But this particular interviewer was new at the job and was convinced that I would resent any question that seemed the least bit prying. This mistaken conviction led her to say at one point: "The next question asks for yearly income. They certainly can't expect many people are going to give me that information. So we'll draw a line through that and go on to the next one." If she had only let me talk, she would have received an accurate answer to the question.

Not wanting to rely entirely on the frankness of his subjects, however, Gurin used several standard procedures for encouraging accurate answers. The interviewers were trained in making it apparent that they were not agreeing or disagreeing with subjects' answers, but simply listening impartially. Also, some of the questions were arranged so as to lead into possibly sensitive topics in a gradual way. For example, some questions about marriage were arranged as follows:

27. First, thinking about a man's (woman's) life—how is a man's (woman's) life changed by being married?

· · ·

30. We've talked a little about marriage in general. Now, thinking about your own marriage, what would you say were the nicest things about it?

31. Every marriage has its good points and bad points. What things about your marriage are not quite as nice as you would like them to be?[3]

The assumption was that a subject is more likely to be frank about the bad aspects of his marriage if the topic is approached gradually than if it is suddenly sprung upon him.

The questionnaire was composed of 108 questions concerning mental health, a few of them borrowed from other studies, but most original. For the most part, questions were read verbatim to the subjects, and their answers were written down verbatim by the interviewers. This process took subjects from one to four hours to complete.

The 2460 completed questionnaires were sent back to the Survey Research Center, where they were analyzed. Some of the major results of those analyses are described here.

SOME RESULTS

The first purpose of the study was to find out how great were the psychological problems of American adults. The question that probably got at the most severe kind of psychological problem was: "Have you ever felt that you were going to have a nervous breakdown?"[4] About 19 per cent of the sample said they had. When these answers were broken down by sex, it was found that 25 per cent of the women but only 12 per cent of the men had answered "yes." This seems consistent with the Thurstones' finding (see Chapter 4) that gender and neuroticism are related.

The study's second purpose was to find out how people react to their psychological problems. One relevant question was: "If something is on your mind that's bothering you or worrying you, and you don't know what to do about it, what do you usually do?"[5] When only the answer each subject mentioned first was counted, the results were as shown in Table 4.

3 Gurin *et al., Americans View Their Mental Health,* pp. 412–13.
4 Gurin *et al., Americans View Their Mental Health,* p. 421.
5 Gurin *et al., Americans View Their Mental Health,* p. 410.

TABLE 4 U.S. ADULTS' FIRST-MENTIONED REACTIONS TO
PROBLEMS*

Reaction	Percent mentioning
Informal help-seeking (talk with friends or relatives)	26
Denial (forget about them; do something to take mind off them)	18
Prayer	16
Do something (think things through; try to change situation)	14
Do nothing at all	10
Keep on worrying (do nothing and problem continues)	6
Formal help-seeking	2
Other	8
Total	100

* After Table 12.1 in G. Gurin, J. Veroff, and Sheila Feld, *Americans View Their Mental Health; A Nationwide Interview Survey* (New York: Basic Books, Inc., Publishers, 1960).

Other questions focused more specifically upon their reactions to seeking professional help:

> Sometimes when people have problems like this [i.e., personal problems], they go someplace for help. Sometimes they go to a doctor or a minister. Sometimes they go to a special place for handling personal problems—like a psychiatrist or a marriage counselor, or social agency or clinic.

> **91.** How about you—have you ever gone anywhere like that for advice and help with any personal problems?

> .   .   .

> **92.** [If answer to 91 was "No."] Can you think of anything that's happened to you, any problems you've had in the past, where going to someone like this might have helped you in any way?[6]

Fourteen per cent (345) of the sample reported that they had gone for help. Nine per cent (220) said they could have used help, but hadn't sought it—because they had worked out their own problems (55 said this), hadn't known how to get help (44), had felt ashamed of their problems (31), hadn't been able to afford help (9), and for other reasons.

The foregoing should give an adequate idea of the results that Gurin and the Joint Commission were mainly concerned with. We, however, want information on an additional topic. We know Freud theorized that conflict is related to anxiety, and that anxiety causes mental avoidance. Let us now see if this survey can offer any hints as to how well these theories fit the normal American adult.

[6] Gurin *et al., Americans View Their Mental Health,* p. 422.

HINTS ABOUT AVOIDANCE AND CONFLICT

To what extent does the average U.S. adult react to problems by mentally or physically avoiding them? Table 4 shows that 18 per cent of Gurin's sample reported they handled worries with techniques that look similar to repression—such as forgetting about them and doing something else to take their minds off them. However, the same table also shows that this was not the most frequent way of dealing with problems. Perhaps normal Americans mentally avoid anxiety-producing problems sometimes, but not as often as Freud's neurotic patients did.

If we were willing to go further into the realm of speculation, we might guess that additional information about the avoidance-anxiety relationship could be gleaned from the answers to the following two questions:

> **86c.** Have you ever been bothered by nervousness, feeling fidgety and tense?
>
> **86f.** Do you find it difficult to get up in the morning?[7]

Subjects answered each of these questions by selecting one of four alternatives: "nearly all the time," "pretty often," "not very much," or "never." These questions and this method of responding were borrowed from another study. If we made the reasonable assumption that the "nervousness" question reflects anxiety and the questionable assumption that "difficulty getting up" often reflects physical avoidance of life's problems by staying in one's warm, safe bed, then we might consider a positive relationship between answers to these questions to support the hypothesis that anxiety and physical avoidance are related.

Gurin calculated this relationship first for men only, and then for women only. The correlation for men was 0.20, and for women, 0.16. While these correlations are not very high, the fact that they are greater than zero suggests some similarity between normal American adults and Freud's patients.

Concerning Freud's hypothesis that anxiety and conflict are related, there is no direct evidence in this study. However, the concept of conflict does come easily to mind as a possible explanation of at least one finding. Why did more women than men report that they had felt, at one time or another, that they were going to have a nervous breakdown? Perhaps American women are more anxious than their husbands because they experience more psychological conflict. The argument would go like this: As women are increasingly encouraged to get an education and

---

[7] Gurin *et al., Americans View Their Mental Health,* p. 420.

take a job, these new goals tend to come in conflict with the more traditional ones of rearing children and keeping house.   Men, in contrast, have little doubt about what their role should be—earning a living for the family.   The greater conflict in women, the argument concludes, might cause them to be more anxious than men.   Whether right or wrong, this kind of argument is quite compatible with Freud's notions about conflict and anxiety.

7 Evaluation of Gurin's Sample Survey

How serious are the psychological problems of the average adult American, and what does he do about them? This seems a worthwhile question, especially when the answers are to guide an attempt to improve the nation's mental health. But how adequately could a study like that of Gurin, Veroff, and Feld answer this question?

Their study is an example of a *sample survey,* a non-experimental study in which information is gathered from a sample of subjects selected to represent a larger group, or population. It is probably fair to say that most sample surveys, including this one, have the following characteristics:

1. Their evidence for accuracy of measurement is moderately strong.
2. Their evidence for generalizability is strong.
3. Their evidence for causality is weak.

ACCURACY OF MEASUREMENT

Reliability. The Survey Research Center trains its interviewers to adopt an objective, scientific attitude and its scorers to follow a scoring system to the letter. This careful training is probably enough to prevent any biases of the survey staff from greatly influencing the results.

No attempt was made in this study to estimate test reliability by asking the same questions twice. However, statistical reliability was estimated and many of the results were found to be statistically significant.

Validity. It is here that the measurements in this study are probably most open to criticism. For example, consider the question, "Have you ever felt that you were going to have a nervous breakdown?" Although this question appears to measure the specified feelings, this appearance may be deceptive. For one thing, some subjects may have once felt that they were going to have a nervous breakdown, but felt it on an unconscious level. Direct questioning—upon which the survey researcher must usually rely—cannot uncover information of which the subject himself is unaware.

Other subjects may not have desired to give truthful answers. As with the Thurstone and Willoughby items, so with Gurin's questions subjects would have little trouble answering so as to make themselves look "good" or "bad" if they wished to do so.

The most effective protection against such possibilities would be direct evidence of validity, but no such evidence was collected in this study.

GENERALIZABILITY

One way to obtain results that are representative of the population of normal American adults would be to interview every single one of them. Although the results of such studies—called *censuses*—are perfectly representative, the cost of conducting them on this large a population is so great that only the federal government can afford it, and only once a decade.

Random sampling. Results that are much less expensive but only slightly less representative can be obtained by interviewing a relatively small representative sample of the population. This is the method Gurin chose. He made sure his sample would be highly representative of the population of U.S. adults in all respects by using random methods to draw the sample from that population.

It should perhaps be mentioned that even random sampling is more expensive than some researchers and pollsters can afford; it takes a lot of time to contact the widely scattered subjects in a sample randomly chosen from a community or nation. For this reason, some surveys are conducted by the interviewer's simply standing on a street corner and interviewing anyone who will stop. Although the low cost of such non-random methods is attractive, there is no assurance that the resulting group of subjects is representative.

Random sampling requires two things: (1) a list that includes every individual in the population and (2) a method of drawing individuals randomly from that list. Due to these two features, every member of the randomly sampled population has an equal chance of being chosen. The same cannot be said of the street-corner type of survey. There, persons who seldom walked past the street corner where the interviewer stood—possibly because they lived in a different part of town, customarily traveled by car instead of by foot, or seldom left their houses—would have little chance of being included in the sample.

If you had twenty subjects—possibly themselves randomly selected from a larger population—and wished to divide them randomly into an experimental and a control group, the list would be a list of the 20 names, and a feasible method of random selection would be drawing names out of a hat.

If you wanted to obtain a sample that was representative of the population of a particular city, you might use as a list an up-to-date city directory, and you might sample names from that list by selecting the first name on every tenth directory page.

Sampling experimental subjects and city residents presents no problems; but what if the population you wished to sample was that of all U.S. adults? Then the usual methods could not be used because it is, practically speaking, impossible to obtain a complete list of U.S. adults. To overcome this difficulty, survey researchers have invented other methods for sampling entire nations. Instead of sampling persons, they sample units of land and interview the persons living on the land units selected. Gurin, for example, used a sampling method which, simplified, was made up of the following steps: (1) from a complete list of U.S. counties, some counties were randomly selected; (2) from these counties, some urban and rural areas were randomly selected; (3) from these urban and rural areas, some houses were randomly selected; and (4) from each of these houses, one adult was randomly selected. This method—called *area sampling*—can produce results equivalent to those that a sampling of individuals would have produced.

A demonstration of random sampling. Taking the example mentioned above of the twenty subjects, suppose that the only thing we knew about them was their names:

> John (10)
> Sam (15)
> Bill (12)
> Orville (8)
> Albert (11)
> Wilbur (14)
> Henry (9)
> Philip (12)
> Ralph (7)

Edward (13)
Nancy (16)
Constance (13)
Jeanne (11)
Mary (14)
Jane (18)
Judy (12)
Ida (15)
Zelda (16)
Helen (21)
Joan (13)

The number beside each name is a hypothetical anxiety score; it is in parentheses to indicate that this information is not available to the researcher.

Before beginning the job of randomly dividing these subjects into two groups, the researcher would probably notice that he did have information about the subjects' "scores" on one variable: sex. It is easy to tell from the names that there are ten boys and ten girls in this group. Since matching usually provides better control than randomization, any variable for which scores are available should be controlled by matching. Here, this means that the male-female ratio should be kept exactly the same—five boys and five girls—in each group. Then randomization will be used to control all other subject variables; that is, *which* five girls and *which* five boys go in each group will be determined by chance alone.

One method of splitting this population is as follows: (1) write each name on a separate slip of paper; (2) put the ten boys' names into a container, shuffle them around, and draw five without looking. The five boys whose names are drawn might go in the experimental group and the five whose names remain, in the control group; (3) put the ten girls' names in the container and proceed as before.

Using this method, I have obtained the two sets of names (and anxiety scores) listed in Table 5. Ordinarily, the researcher would not have scores on a randomized variable available to him (because if the scores were available, he would have used matching, not randomization, to control the variable) and therefore would not be able to find out exactly how good a job of control randomization had done. In this case, however, we can see that the experimental group has a mean anxiety score of 13.4, and the control group, a mean score of 12.6. Although randomization has not controlled anxiety perfectly, the difference between the two group means (0.8) is not very far from zero.

If you applied the same name-drawing procedure to these same subjects several times, you would find that the difference in anxiety between the experimental and control groups varied somewhat; however, in most cases the differences would be rather small.

TABLE 5   GROUPS RESULTING FROM A RANDOM ASSIGNMENT
OF SUBJECTS

Experimental group		Control group	
Name	Anxiety score	Name	Anxiety score
John	10	Albert	11
Orville	8	Wilbur	14
Henry	9	Philip	12
Bill	12	Sam	15
Edward	13	Ralph	7
Jane	18	Judy	12
Mary	14	Constance	13
Nancy	16	Zelda	16
Helen	21	Jeanne	11
Joan	13	Ida	15
Mean:	13.4	Mean:	12.6

Randomization and the estimation of statistical reliability. Any variable
(except the variable being measured) that affects a measurement and
that varies randomly will produce random error in that measurement.
The more random error in a measure, the less reliable it is.

Variables that are perfectly controlled by the methods of holding
constant and matching do not contribute to random error. But variables
that are controlled by randomization—and they must be numerous in
any study—continue to provide a certain amount of random error. This
is because randomization never provides perfect control, no matter how
many subjects are used.

To see the problem raised by the existence of random error, suppose
that the two groups in Table 5 were used in a study on anxiety. The experimental group received a treatment intended to arouse anxiety, while
the control group received no such treatment. At the end of the experiment the investigator found that the one group obtained a mean anxiety
score of 13.4, and the other group, a mean score of 12.6. Not knowing, as
we do, that this difference existed even before the treatments were administered, this experimenter could not be absolutely certain that it was not
at least partly due to the independent variable. He could, however, estimate the likelihood that this was so. Applying an appropriate statistical
formula, he would find that the probability was greater than .30 that the
obtained difference was due entirely to random error. Since this probability is too large for comfort, being much larger than the commonly
accepted criterion of .05, the experimenter would decide, in this case, correctly, that he could not conclude that the difference was reliable.

CAUSALITY

The survey researcher has no particular trouble detecting relationships between variables, but he does have difficulty telling cause from effect because his surveys seldom permit him to manipulate independent variables or to use randomization to control extraneous variables.

Relationships. Gurin looked for and found relationships between many pairs of variables. For one example, he wanted to find out how strong a direct causal relationship existed between "nervousness" and "difficulty getting up in the morning." But unless precautions were taken, at least one extraneous variable—sex—might artificially inflate the obtained relationship. That is, if nervousness and difficulty both happened to be related to gender (or any other variable), this alone would make them related to each other, even if neither was causing the other. As mentioned in Chapter 1, the way to make sure that a relationship reflects only the direct causal connections between the two variables is to control the extraneous variable or variables—in this case, sex.

Control. To control the sex variable by matching, one could assign subjects in such a way that the ratio of men to women was the same in each nervousness group. This is essentially what Gurin did when he computed the nervousness-difficulty relationship first for men only and then for women only.

While no critic can complain that sex was not controlled in the analysis of this particular relationship, it was the only variable controlled. Since Gurin had to choose the groups on the basis of their reported nervousness, he could not select them randomly and thus could not gain the blanket control of subject variables which randomization provides. Thus Gurin has little protection against such arguments as the one that age might have produced the obtained nervousness-difficulty relationships. For example, if old age caused nervousness and also difficulty getting up in the morning, this would make nervousness and difficulty related even if neither was causing the other. This particular argument may be groundless, but the important point is that Gurin has no evidence against it.

Order. Since Gurin could not manipulate any of the variables, he had only common sense to tell him which of two related variables changed first. In the case of the relationship between sex and feelings of impending nervous breakdown, it seems obvious that the sex difference existed

first.   But in other cases, such as that of the nervousness-difficulty relationship, common sense provides no sure indication of order.   It could
be that nervousness makes people reluctant to get up, it could be that
people who consistently oversleep become nervous that they might lose
their jobs, or it could be both.

In summary, the inability of the survey researcher to manipulate independent variables, while it does not prevent him from discovering relationships or controlling variables through matching, does make it
impossible for him to control subject variables through randomization,
or to obtain the most convincing kind of evidence about which variable
changed first.

If surveys and other non-experimental studies have so many weaknesses, you may ask, why don't all investigators do experiments instead?
The answer is that experiments, while they do avoid some of the weaknesses of the survey, have their own weaknesses.   This will become
apparent in Chapters 8 and 10, which describe some experiments on conflict and avoidance.

8 Pavlov and Miller
Experiment on Conflict

As we have seen, Freud's explorations of his patients' problems led him to consider conflict a crucial factor in neurosis. His eventual view on this matter is indicated in the following passage:

> In these people [persons who suddenly fall ill of a neurosis] signs of contradictory and opposed wishes, or, as we say, of *mental conflict*, are regularly found. One side of the personality stands for certain wishes, while another part struggles against them and fends them off. There is no neurosis without such a CONFLICT.[1]

Could it be that the reason conflict is so closely related to neurosis is that it *causes* neurosis? Freud's evidence for this and other causal hypotheses was far from complete. This is because he relied primarily on the non-experimental case study, whereas it is the experiment which provides the best evidence for causality. Several experiments on conflict are described in this chapter, and several others related to repression and avoidance are described in Chapter 10.

Like many other concepts used by Freud, the concept of conflict has continued to interest more recent psychologists, even some of those who are committed to the principles of behaviorism, which are at odds with some of the research methods Freud used.

[1] Sigmund Freud, *A General Introduction to Psychoanalysis,* trans. Joan Riviere (Garden City, N.Y.: Garden City Publishing Co., 1920), p. 305. Used by permission of the Liveright Publishing Co., New York.

Behaviorism, a viewpoint officially "founded" by the American psychologist John Watson in 1913, was a reaction against the practice, common among psychologists of Freud's day, of taking at face value subjects' reports of their own feelings, perceptions, and other mental processes. One of the main reasons the early behaviorists objected to this practice was that they felt such self-reports were of doubtful objectivity. Furthermore, they thought that their objectivity could not be checked because no one else can look inside a person's mind. For these and other reasons, the behaviorists recommended that psychologists restrict their method to observing overt stimuli and behavior, which seemed more objectively measurable. This basic recommendation—which has been widely followed, especially by U.S. psychologists—stands virtually unchanged today, although some of the details of the behavioristic viewpoint have been modified.

Two of the major figures associated with behaviorism—the Russian, Ivan Pavlov, and the American, Clark Hull—are discussed in this chapter because they and their students have contributed to the understanding of conflict.

PAVLOV'S DISCOVERY OF EXPERIMENTAL NEUROSIS[2]

Ivan Pavlov was so completely devoted to his physiological research that sometimes his wife even had to remind him that it was time to go and collect his salary. As a result of this devotion, the research carried out in his St. Petersburg laboratory was excellent. In fact, his early studies on the secretion of the digestive glands of dogs won a Nobel Prize.

In the course of this research, Pavlov happened to notice an interesting thing: the dogs would begin to salivate when the lab assistant who ordinarily fed them approached, even if he brought no food. It was as if the dogs had learned to "expect" food whenever they saw the assistant.

Further work has shown that this is a general sort of occurrence. When a neutral stimulus (conditioned stimulus) is repeatedly paired with a stimulus (unconditioned stimulus) that elicits a particular response (unconditioned response), that neutral stimulus will come to elicit a similar response (conditioned response). This is customarily diagrammed as in Figure 2. This procedure for producing learning—which came to be called *classical conditioning*—appealed to the behaviorists because all the elements involved are relatively easy to observe objectively.

2 The material in this section is based largely on Ivan Pavlov, *Conditioned Reflexes*, trans. G. V. Anrep (London: Oxford University Press, 1927). Used by permission of the Clarendon Press, Oxford.

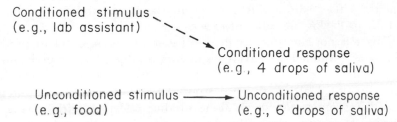

FIGURE 2 Recipe for classical or Pavlovian conditioning: Present a neutral stimulus to subject. About a half-second later, present another stimulus which consistently produces (solid arrow) a response. Repeat this procedure for many trials. The result should be a gradually increasing tendency for the originally neutral stimulus itself to produce (broken line indicates this "connection" is learned) a response similar to the unconditioned one.

Pavlov himself became so interested in this learning process that, shortly after 1900, he steered his students' research away from the topic of digestion and toward a wide variety of topics related to classical conditioning. Some of these studies led, rather unexpectedly, to findings concerning conflict. Such a study is described here.

One of Pavlov's students set out to use classical conditioning to find out how small a difference between two shapes a dog could detect. He did this by first projecting a circle of light on a screen in front of the animal, and at the same moment feeding it. After the salivary response had become well conditioned to the circle, the experimenter began presenting a luminous ellipse instead of the circle on some of the trials. The ellipse was not accompanied by food and therefore the dog—as long as it could tell the two shapes apart—would salivate to the circle but not to the ellipse. Thus classical conditioning had provided the dog with a signal—salivation—by which it informed the experimenter whether it could distinguish circle from ellipse.

The next step in the study was to see how similar the ellipse could be made to the circle before the animal failed to tell them apart. The ellipse was gradually made more circular until the dog was unable to tell the two shapes apart consistently, even with three weeks of training. When training on the same difficult ellipse continued beyond three weeks, the animal's ability to distinguish it from the circle declined and eventually disappeared completely. At the same time, to the experimenter's surprise, the formerly quiet dog began to bark violently when led into the training room at the beginning of each experimental session, and to squeal, wriggle about, and bite at the experimental apparatus during the sessions. Furthermore, when the experimenter went back and tested this dog on the easiest ellipse, the animal now could not distinguish even it from the circle. Since this experimentally produced behavior looked neurotic to Pavlov, he called it *experimental neurosis.*

This was not the only set of conditions that was found to produce "neurosis." Another of Pavlov's students conducted an experiment in which strong electric shock and food were presented at the same time. When presented alone, the two stimuli had produced quite different kinds of responses: the shock alone produced fearful, withdrawing behavior (a defense reaction), whereas food alone produced eating behavior (an alimentary reaction). It was of some interest, then, to find out which response would become conditioned to which stimulus when both stimuli were presented together. At first the alimentary reaction gained the upper hand and became conditioned to the shock. That is, after conditioning, shock alone produced no defense reaction, but only salivation, smacking of the lips, and looking in the direction from which food usually came. Then the experimenter began to apply the shock to other parts of the dog's body to see if the salivary response would *generalize,* or spread to the slightly different stimuli. At first the shocks continued to produce salivation even when applied at the new body locations. However,

> When a still further place was added to those already successfully generalized everything underwent an abrupt and complete change. No trace of the alimentary reaction was left: instead only a most violent defense reaction was present. Even an extremely weak current, which before the development of the alimentary conditioned reflex remained entirely without effect, now when applied to the original place of stimulation or to any other brought about the most violent defense reaction.[3]

This procedure was carried out with three dogs, and in each case the resulting "neurosis" was long-lasting.

Although the circle-ellipse study and the food-shock study were quite different in their details, you have probably noticed similarities between them. For one thing, both studies seem to involve conflict. Pavlov put it like this:

> Broadly we can regard these disturbances as due to a conflict between the processes of excitation and inhibition which the cortex [the brain's gray matter] finds difficult to resolve.[4]

That is, Pavlov was speculating that in the early stages of the first experiment the circle produced an excitatory tendency (a tendency to make

[3] Pavlov, *Conditioned Reflexes,* p. 290.
[4] Pavlov, *Conditioned Reflexes,* p. 302.

a salivary response) and the ellipse produced an inhibitory tendency (a tendency not to make that response). When circle and ellipse were made so similar that the dog could no longer tell them apart, both excitatory and inhibitory tendencies occurred simultaneously to the circle and simultaneously to the ellipse. This direct conflict of opposing tendencies somehow led to neurotic behavior. Pavlov thought that something similar happened in the food-shock study.

As previously mentioned, the ability to manipulate a variable can have important research advantages. These studies by Pavlov's students, since they appeared to demonstrate how neurosis could be manipulated, seemed to lay the foundation for great progress in the understanding of neurosis. For some reason, however, research on experimental neurosis has not yet produced the breakthroughs that many had anticipated.

HULL'S BEHAVIOR THEORY

Another line of research and theory which has led to work on conflict is that of Clark Hull. Hull had a strong theoretical bent; he enjoyed searching out fundamental principles. This inclination once caused him to consider entering the ministry, but he disliked the thought of having to attend numerous ladies' teas. So he turned to psychology and the search for fundamental laws of behavior. The extensive theoretical system which Hull eventually developed—largely while he was research professor at Yale University—has had a great influence upon psychology. However, only those of his principles that are most relevant to conflict will be outlined here. These principles can best be illustrated in terms of the situation which Hull often used in his experiments—that of a rat in an alley which is just wide enough for it to run down and which sometimes contains food at the far end or "goal." Hull thought that the strength of the rat's tendency to run toward the goal is affected by:

1. The amount of habit or learned tendency the animal has to run toward the goal in that situation. The amount of approach habit is greater, Hull thought, the more times the rat has previously run to the goal and been *reinforced* or rewarded for it—perhaps by finding food there. Notice that this kind of learning, often called *instrumental conditioning,* is at least superficially different from classical conditioning.

2. The amount of drive or motive the rat has. For example, a rat that had just gone ten hours without food would—if some approach habit were present—run faster than one that had gone hungry only four hours.

3. The distance of the rat from the goal. The closer the rat is to the goal, the stronger the tendency to run toward it (if approach habit and drive are present). This means that as the rat approached the goal, it would move faster

and faster; presumably, you and I do the same sort of thing as we near the supper table in the evening.

MILLER'S APPLICATION OF HULL'S THEORY TO CONFLICT

Neal Miller studied under Hull at Yale and joined the Yale faculty upon receiving his Ph.D. there.   Whereas Hull did most of his theorizing about instances where only one response tendency is present, Miller wondered what would happen if two conflicting response tendencies occurred at the same time.   More concretely, what would happen if a rat that had been trained to approach a goal received a shock when it pushed its snout into the food trough at the end of the alley?   That shock would be expected to create—on top of the already-existing tendency to approach the goal— a conflicting tendency to avoid it.

Applying Hull's principles to this more complex situation, Miller made the following assumptions:[5]

1. The tendency to approach a goal is stronger the nearer the subject is to it. This is the third of Hull's principles mentioned above and is graphically represented by the slope of the solid line in Figure 3.

2. The tendency to avoid a feared stimulus is stronger the nearer the subject is to it.   This is the same Hullian principle applied to avoidance and is represented by the slope of the broken line in Figure 3.

3. The strength of avoidance increases more rapidly with nearness to the goal than does that of approach.   This is a new assumption and is graphically represented in Figure 3 by the fact that the broken line has a steeper slope than the solid line.

4. The strength of the approach or avoidance tendency can be changed by appropriate changes in the relevant habits or drives.   That is, if Hull was right that any response tendency is determined by habit and drive, then the approach and avoidance tendencies can be raised or lowered by appropriate increases or decreases in habit or drive.

5. When two incompatible responses are in conflict, the stronger will occur.

6. Assumptions 1–5 apply not only to physical distance from a goal, but also to perceived dissimilarity to a goal-object.   In other words, the same kinds of changes in response tendencies that occur when a rat moves further away from a goal will also occur as the rat confronts a series of objects that are less and less similar to an original goal-object.   This is illustrated in Figure 4.

[5] These assumptions are from N. Miller, "Liberalization of Basic S-R Concepts: Extensions to Conflict Behavior, Motivation, and Social Learning," in S. Koch, ed., *Psychology: A Study of a Science, II* (New York: McGraw-Hill Book Company, 1959), 205–6.

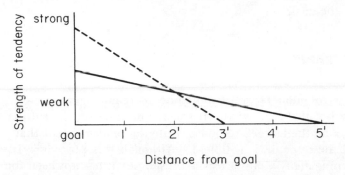

FIGURE 3 Approach-avoidance conflict; strength of tendencies to approach (solid line) and avoid (broken line) as a function of distance from goal. The distance units used are merely illustrative. At 2 units from goal, the conflicting tendencies are of equal strength.

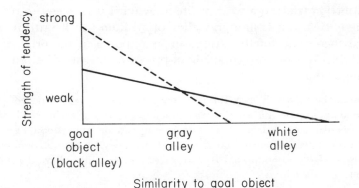

FIGURE 4 Approach-avoidance conflict; strength of tendencies to approach (solid line) and avoid (broken line) as a function of similarity to goal object.

Several predictions can be derived from this set of assumptions. The prediction of greatest relevance here is the following: If the lines representing the approach and avoidance tendencies cross, the subject will be "trapped" at the crossing point, because this is the only point where the opposing tendencies are of equal strength; at all other points, either the approach or the avoidance tendency is stronger, forcing the subject toward the crossing point. Miller has tested this hypothesis using rats in alleys and has obtained some results which support it.

If the rat is trapped at the crossing point, wanting the food at the goal yet fearing the shock it expects there, and the experimenter then shuts off the shocking device, the animal is in a situation similar to that of a neurotic human. The fear which thwarts its desire is now irrational.

How can this irrational avoidance tendency be reduced to permit the rat to reach the goal?

"RAT THERAPY"

The most common laboratory method of removing a learned response tendency is called *extinction*. It consists of allowing the subject to continue making the learned response while the reinforcement that formerly followed the response is withheld. Although this procedure is effective in weakening many kinds of learned responses, it has not been found very effective in removing learned avoidance responses.

There is a more roundabout extinction procedure, however, which Miller's theory implies might remove the rat's conflict more quickly: If the alley in which the conflict was learned was narrow and black, run the rat's first extinction trials in a wide, white alley until it manages to reach the goal there; then run it in a gray alley of medium width until it reaches the goal there; and finally extinguish its response in the original black alley. Miller thought this roundabout procedure might be helpful for the following reasons:

1. It should be relatively easy for the "neurotic" rat to reach the goal in the white alley because this alley is very dissimilar to the alley in which the conflict was originally learned. This reasoning can be understood by studying Figure 4. There, when the rat is in the black alley, avoidance predominates. However, if the same animal is transferred to the white alley, the approach tendency predominates.

2. After the rat reaches the goal of the white alley and experiences no shock, its avoidance tendency will extinguish somewhat and this extinction will generalize to the gray and black alleys. Then it runs the gray alley and reaching the goal there produces further extinction of the avoidance tendency. When the rat is finally returned to the black alley, the extinction that has already occurred makes it relatively easy for the animal to reach the black goal and thus complete the extinction of the fear response it learned there earlier. It seems possible, although not certain, that this roundabout procedure would produce complete extinction of the avoidance tendency in a shorter number of trials than the direct procedure of simply continuing to run the rat in the black alley.

To check on this theorizing, Mitchell Berkun, one of Miller's graduate students at Yale, carried out an experiment which followed the above plan.[6] He first trained each of 64 male rats to run down a black alley for

---

[6] Besides omitting many details of Berkun's study, I have oversimplified it on one point. The impression is given here that all rats received their original training in the black alley; actually some were trained in the white alley, and the roundabout extinction procedure went from black alley to gray alley to white alley.

food; next he gave each animal three trials in which, upon touching the food container, it received a shock. Then the shocking device was disconnected, and half the rats "recovered" from their fear by running all their extinction trials in the black alley, while the other half ran the white-gray-black procedure described above. The numbers of trials it took the two groups to reach the various goals are indicated in Table 6. The rats running only in the black alley took a mean of 12.6 trials to reach the black goal. The roundabout group tended to take fewer trials (mean, 9.4) to reach the white goal; this finding supported one of Miller's hypotheses. To reach the black goal, however, the roundabout group took somewhat longer (mean, 15 trials) than their comrades.

TABLE 6 EFFECTS OF ROUNDABOUT AND DIRECT EXTINCTION PROCEDURES*

Mean number of trials to reach goals

Procedure	White	Gray	Black	Total
Roundabout	9.4	3.0	2.6	15
Direct			12.6	12.6

* After M. M. Berkun, "Factors in the Recovery from Approach-Avoidance Conflict," *Journal of Experimental Psychology*, LIV (1957), 65–73.

The fact that the more roundabout extinction procedure was not advantageous in this experiment does not necessarily mean that it couldn't be in other circumstances. One would expect the relative effectiveness of this kind of procedure to vary from situation to situation, depending on such factors as the nature of the conflict and the similarity of the other "alleys" used.

9 Evaluation of the Pavlov and Miller Experiments

If conflict plays as crucial a part in neurosis as Freud thought, it is an extremely important topic to study. The major practical goal of such research would of course be to learn how to destroy neurosis. It is to the credit of the studies described in the previous chapter, then, that they seem to be steps toward this goal. Pavlov's work shows that neurotic behavior can be caused by at least some kinds of conflict, and Miller's theory suggests some ways in which conflict might be reduced.

All three studies described in Chapter 8 were laboratory experiments. You will recall that an experiment is a study in which one or more independent variables are manipulated; often this is possible only in the laboratory. Laboratory experiments typically have the following characteristics:

1. Their evidence for accuracy of measurement is strong.
2. Their evidence for generalizability is weak, in the opinion of many.
3. Their evidence for causality is strong.

A comparison of the characteristics of the experiment with those of the sample survey (p. 44) shows that each method is strong where the other is weak.

ACCURACY OF MANIPULATION

Although this topic ordinarily receives little attention, it is worth mentioning that experimental manipulation, like measurement, faces the problems of reliability and validity. For example, how reliably and how validly were Pavlov and Berkun creating conflict in their subjects?

Inconsistency of a manipulated variable will contribute to the inconsistency of an influenced dependent variable and thus be reflected in the reliability estimates for the latter.

The validity of a manipulation is often judged on appearances alone —that is, does it appear that the intended variable is in fact the one being manipulated? Methods of construct validation may also be used: if it is hypothesized that conflict causes neurosis, and if it is then found that what is intended as a manipulation of conflict does influence what is intended as a measure of neurosis, this finding is some evidence that the manipulation, as well as the measure, is valid.

ACCURACY OF MEASUREMENT

While little criticism can be made of Berkun's measures, the same is not true of some of Pavlov's observations. Perhaps this is due to the fact that Pavlov's work on experimental neurosis was exploratory in nature.

Reliability. It was no accident that Berkun's experiment required him to measure only such variables as the number of trials it took subjects to reach various goals. Berkun focused on such variables partly because they required virtually no subjective judgments of the observer and therefore could be measured with high objectivity. If he had attempted to measure such variables as "eagerness to reach the goal" or "amount of fear," on the other hand, he would have been on more dangerous ground.

One important measurement taken by Pavlov's students was undoubtedly also highly objective—the measurement of the salivary response. There might be some doubt, however, concerning the objectivity of their observations of the "violent" barking in the first study and the "violent" defense reaction in the second. It seems quite possible that if other observers had been present, they might have judged the barking to be "continuous" or "loud" or "frightened," instead of "violent."

Objectivity probably would have been higher if Pavlov had attempted to measure only such aspects of the neurotic reactions as "frequency of barks." However, since experimental neurosis was just being discovered, Pavlov was probably wise to report everything he observed about it, whether objectively measurable or not.

To turn to other aspects of reliability, only one of Berkun's results for the "trials" measure was found to be statistically significant. Whereas the black-alley goal was attained by the "direct" group in a mean of 12.6 trials, it was reached by the "roundabout" group after a mean of only 2.6 trials in the black alley. The estimated likelihood that a mean difference this large would occur due to random error alone is considerably less than .05.

Pavlov, apparently not much concerned with maximizing reliability, used very few subjects in each of the described studies. Perhaps this was because he was accustomed to studying physiological processes like digestion, which are virtually identical in the majority of subjects. When he turned to the study of classical conditioning, however, he probably should have paid more attention to the problem of reliability; at least it is a common opinion that psychological processes are generally less consistent than physiological ones.

Validity. Berkun used the number of trials it took a rat to reach a goal as a measure of the speed with which that animal's avoidance tendencies extinguished. If we accept Miller's conflict theory, we can be fairly confident that progress toward a goal did validly reflect extinction rather than some other process.

That is, Miller's theory says that the main factors that can bring a conflicted rat to move closer to a goal are (1) an increase in the approach tendency, or (2) a decrease in (extinction of) the avoidance tendency. The approach tendency could increase due to an increase in the amount of habit to approach, or due to an increase in drive (in this case, hunger). But Berkun controlled all these factors except extinction of the avoidance tendency. On most extinction trials he prevented approach habit from increasing by making sure no reward was present. He held hunger constant from session to session. Therefore, assuming the theory is correct, the major factor responsible for the rat's progress toward a goal must have been exactly what Berkun wanted to measure—extinction of the avoidance tendency.

Pavlov thought he was measuring neurosis. While he might easily have been wrong, this would not be a very serious error in this particular case. Pavlov was not in the usual position of having in mind a variable and then trying to find a measure of it; in such cases, it is crucial that the measure adopted be a valid one. Quite the reverse, Pavlov had hit upon some measures which gave interesting results, and his only problem was to name them. This is not to say that there would be no value in knowing whether the canine behavior Pavlov observed was, in some sense, truly neurotic. But that was a task that could easily wait for others.

GENERALIZABILITY

Perhaps one of the most common criticisms that has been made of laboratory experimentation concerns generalizability. Few experimenters make much attempt to study stimuli, subjects, or responses that are closely representative of any situation of practical importance.

Experimental psychologists might protest that they are not interested in generalizing their results, that the psychological principles they study are so basic that they can be generalized even if closely representative subjects were not used, or that it is impossible to bring certain kinds of situations into the laboratory.

These defenses are not likely to silence the critics. For one thing, they would complain that Pavlov's and Berkun's use of animal subjects makes it risky to generalize their findings to humans. This is because humans differ from lower animals on many variables, one of the most important of which is ability to use language. There are many methods of measuring and treating human anxiety that use language, and animal studies cannot, of course, provide much evidence regarding such methods.

Nor is human research entirely safe from such criticism, since most human subjects are drawn from a rather special group—that of college students enrolled in introductory psychology courses.

As a result, such critics would say, much guesswork is often required in generalizing the results of laboratory studies. This guesswork need not, however, be blind. It would be reasonable to argue, for example, that findings obtained from college students are more likely to apply to other college students, other young adults, and other members of the middle class than to persons outside those categories.

CAUSALITY

Relationships. Like every other kind of study, the laboratory experiment can provide evidence for relationships. For example, Pavlov's circle-ellipse study showed a relationship between similarity of shapes, on the one hand, and the dog's salivation, squealing, wriggling, and barking, on the other. His shock-food study showed a relationship between the shifting of the location of shock and the disappearance of the conditioned salivary response. One relationship shown by Berkun's experiment was that between the extinction procedure used and the number of trials spent in the black alley.

Control. All the different methods of control are illustrated in these experiments. Holding constant was used by Pavlov to control shock intensity, and by Berkun to control the amount of avoidance training his rats received. Using the subject as his own control occurred in both of the Pavlov studies. We might say that, in the one study, the same dog was in all the "similarity of shape" conditions, and that, in the other, the same subjects were in all the "location of shock" conditions. Matching was used by Berkun to control species, strain, and sex of subjects. Finally, Berkun used randomization to control all additional characteristics of his subjects. Randomization, you will recall, is the only one of these control techniques which is not also available in non-experimental studies.

Order. Could anyone suppose that Pavlov's dogs first became neurotic, for some unknown reason, and then, perhaps in the course of their neurotic behavior, pawed a switch which made the ellipse more similar to the circle? No, because the experimenter was the one changing the ellipse. If neurosis couldn't have caused similarity of shape, it must have been similarity of shape that caused neurosis (assuming, as always, that all extraneous variables were adequately controlled).

In Berkun's study, could those rats that were destined to extinguish rapidly somehow have decided to run the black-alley procedure? No, because the experimenter assigned subjects to procedures. If a rat's extinction speed couldn't have determined which extinction procedure he underwent, the only remaining possibility is that the extinction procedure determined speed of extinction.

THE IDEAL THAT THEORY BE GENERAL

Some think that psychological theory should be as general as possible, that is, that the theorist should attempt to explain the largest possible number of facts with the smallest possible number of theoretical statements. Although there seems to be little disagreement that this should be an eventual goal of psychology, there are those who feel that researchers have not yet collected enough basic facts to begin this theoretical task.

Clark Hull, however, felt even in the 1930's that it was not too early to start building general theories. His behavior theory, of which only a small segment was described in Chapter 8, was in part an attempt to integrate many behavior principles into one general theoretical framework. Once this theory was constructed, Hull and his students and colleagues attempted to extend it—adding to the theory when necessary—to previously unexplained kinds of behavior.

Miller's work on conflict was one notable attempt to extend Hull's theory to a new topic and thereby to increase its generality.

ETHICS IN RESEARCH

Pavlov and Berkun created fear in their animal subjects. Was this ethically justified?

Most psychological studies cause subjects some "inconvenience." In the human studies of Willoughby and Gurin, this involved little more than taking up subjects' time. When more severe "inconveniences" such as food deprivation or pain are required, researchers usually resort to animal subjects.

For every study, a decision must be made as to whether the benefits likely to be gained by the subjects and by society are worth the particular inconveniences imposed on subjects. In human research, both the investigator (or some other "objective" person) and the subject—by choosing whether or not to participate—have customarily made this decision. In fact, one government agency—the U.S. Public Health Service—has recently made it a requirement that every investigator applying for human research funds must first have the ethical aspects of his research design approved by a group of his colleagues. This group must make sure that the rights of subjects will be protected and that subjects will be given a meaningful choice whether or not to participate.

In animal research the investigator, although to some extent limited by law, has for the most part made the ethical decisions himself. Apparently Berkun and Pavlov felt that the possible value of their studies did justify the shocks and other traumatic stimuli they used. Others might disagree with them.

10 Mowrer and Solomon Experiment on Avoidance

Whereas the previous two chapters dealt with experimental work on conflict, the experiments discussed in this chapter and the next are relevant to Freud's concept of repression. Strictly speaking, these are experiments on physical avoidance. However, it seems likely that repression and avoidance have something in common; while repression prevents conscious mental contact with painful ideas, avoidance prevents physical contact with painful physical stimuli.

Why do anxiety and avoidance, once established, last so excruciatingly long? Although Freud raised this question, he could not answer it. To understand the problem, suppose that a small boy has taken to running into the house whenever he sees a dog approaching, because on several previous occasions he was attacked by a dog. Common sense might say that this is a case of simple classical conditioning, where the sight of a dog is the conditioned stimulus, the attack is the unconditioned stimulus, and running into the house is the conditioned response. But if this were so, when the boy began running into the house quickly enough to avoid the attacks, the unconditioned stimulus would no longer be experienced and, for this reason, the avoidance response should extinguish rather quickly. The fact of the matter is, however, that avoidance behavior can extinguish very slowly.

Little progress was made in fathoming this problem until the 1940's—over 30 years after the nonsense of little Hans—when Orval Hobart Mowrer, a member of the Yale circle which included Hull and Miller, became interested in it. Mowrer's interest in the phenomena of neurosis was more than academic. He himself suffered intermittent attacks of neurotic depression for many years. In fact, he says that it was his own symptoms that led him into his profession: "I was going to have to study this thing called Psychology and find out, if I could, what . . . was the matter *with me*."[1]

When the attacks continued, Mowrer underwent several periods of psychoanalysis. In this way he, unlike many who are trained in the tradition of behaviorism or stimulus-response psychology, became very familiar with Freud's work. In much of his subsequent research, Mowrer attempted to use behavioristic concepts (such as classical and instrumental conditioning) to improve upon Freud's theories.

MOWRER'S TWO-FACTOR THEORY

In an attempt to explain how avoidance behavior can extinguish so slowly, Mowrer developed his two-factor theory, so-called because it states that both classical and instrumental conditioning are factors in avoidance learning.

Both these types of conditioning occur in the earliest stage of avoidance learning, that stage when the subject experiences the unpleasant stimulus and then escapes from it. First, because the boy sees a dog and at the same time feels the pain of teeth biting his leg, he learns to fear the sight of dogs. This is classical conditioning. Next comes a particularly crucial hypothesis—that this learned fear (or, more exactly, its reduction) is partly responsible for the learning of the avoidance (running) response. That is, when the boy runs away from the attacking dog and into his house, his fear decreases, and this fear reduction reinforces his running behavior; as a result, he learns to run into the house whenever he sees a dog. This is instrumental conditioning. This much of the theory is diagrammed in Figure 5.

If the theory is correct so far, what should happen when the boy begins to respond so quickly to the sight of an approaching dog that he reaches safety before any attack can occur? Since the attack was the unconditioned stimulus in the classical conditioning of fear, fear should now begin to extinguish. The boy's running response, on the other hand, was not completely dependent upon the canine attacks. To some extent, his running depended upon the learned fear response, which continues to occur, although more and more weakly, since it is in the process of extin-

[1] O. H. Mowrer, "Abnormal Reactions or Actions?" in J. A. Vernon, ed., *Introduction to General Psychology* (Dubuque, Iowa: W. C. Brown Company Publishers, 1966), p. 8.

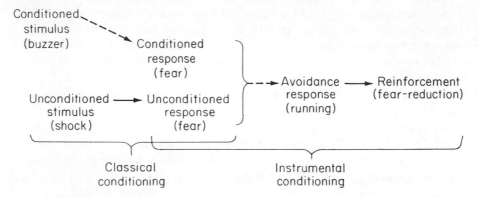

FIGURE 5 Mowrer's two-factor theory of avoidance conditioning. Broken arrows indicate "connections" which are gradually learned. Solid arrows indicate "connections" which exist from the very beginning of conditioning.

guishing.   Therefore the boy's running response, instead of immediately beginning to extinguish, will actually continue to be reinforced for some time after he stops experiencing the dog's attacks.

At some point, however, the boy's fear of the dog will reach complete extinction; when that happens, the avoidance response can be reinforced no longer, and it too will begin to extinguish.

Mowrer did not appear to claim that extinction of either the fear or the avoidance response was unusually slow.   He claimed only that avoidance behavior takes an unusually long time to extinguish because it has to wait for fear to extinguish completely before it can even begin its own extinction.

If Mowrer's theory were correct, it might possibly help to explain the observation that Hans continued to avoid horses for four months.   But was it correct?   Particularly, was the central hypothesis that avoidance behavior is reinforced by fear reduction correct?

MOWRER'S EXPERIMENT[2]

How could one find out if fear reduction reinforces avoidance behavior? Mowrer hit upon the idea of testing this hypothesis by making use of a widely accepted principle of learning.   This was the principle that in in-

---

[2] The material in this section is based largely on O. H. Mowrer and R. R. Lamoreaux, "Avoidance Conditioning and Signal Duration—A Study of Secondary Motivation and Reward," *Psychological Monographs*, LIV, No. 247 (1942).

strumental conditioning the sooner the reinforcement occurs after the response, the more learning occurs. If a reinforcement occurs at the same moment the subject makes the response, learning will be strongest; if a reinforcement occurs some time after or some time before the response, learning will be weaker.

According to this principle, if fear reduction in fact reinforces avoidance behavior, then *when* fear reduction occurs during avoidance training should affect learning.

To test this prediction, Mowrer—by then at Harvard University—and a student, Ross R. Lamoreaux, performed a laboratory experiment. They obtained twenty-one female and three male rats, all of the same genetic strain and approximately the same age, and all reared in a laboratory to ensure ignorance of experimental tasks. These rats were assigned to three groups, each containing seven females and one male; although the report does not state that this assignment was random, it seems likely that it was.

In every respect but one, the three groups of rats were treated exactly alike. Every day each rat was taken out of its cage, carried into the soundproofed experimental room, set down on one end of the steel floor of a long, narrow box, and left there a few moments to reconnoiter. Then an unseen buzzer sounded, and exactly five seconds later the half of the floor upon which the rat was crouching became charged with electricity. The rat jumped about, tried to climb the walls, and sooner or later reached the opposite, non-electrified end of the box. It had escaped the painful shock for the time being. A short while later, the buzzer sounded again, this time followed (again, five seconds later) by electrification of that half of the floor upon which the rat was now standing. On this second trial it probably took the animal slightly less time to scramble to the safe end of the box. Sooner or later the rat was running so promptly when the buzzer sounded that it reached the safe side before the shock came on. When this happened, the animal was no longer escaping from the shock, but avoiding it entirely. This learning process parallels closely the example of the boy learning to avoid dogs.

The one way in which Mowrer's three groups were treated differently was that the buzzer, which always started at the same relative moment, *stopped* at different moments. Why was this done? Remember that the variable Mowrer wished to manipulate was *when* fear reduction occurred. Since the rats would quickly learn to fear the buzzer, Mowrer reasoned, he could reduce fear at different moments by shutting off the feared buzzer at different moments. For the "before" group, the buzzer always stopped one second after it had begun, which was nearly always before escape or avoidance could occur; for the "simultaneous" group, the buzzer stopped at exactly the same instant the rat crossed to the safe side of the box; and for the "after" group, the buzzer stopped five seconds after the rat had reached safe territory. According to his theory, Mowrer expected that, in a given number of trials, the "simultaneous" group would show more avoidance learning than either the "before" or the "after" group.

During the study, the experimenter kept a record sheet on which he noted, for each trial, whether or not the rat succeeded in avoiding the shock. Each rat's total number of avoidances in 100 trials is indicated in Table 7. The finding that the simultaneous group achieved the highest mean number of avoidance trials supported Mowrer's theory.

TABLE 7 NUMBER OF TRIALS INDIVIDUAL RATS AVOIDED SHOCK*

"Before" group	"Simultaneous" group	"After" group
31	64	22
39	74	23
49	79	28
51	80	53
57	86	58
61	91	60
74	93	63
78	94	65
Mean: $440/8 = 55$	$661/8 = 82.6$	$372/8 = 46.5$

* After O. H. Mowrer and R. R. Lamoreaux, "Avoidance Conditioning and Signal Duration—A Study of Secondary Motivation and Reward," *Psychological Monographs*, LIV, No. 247 (1942).

SOLOMON'S EXPERIMENT[3]

The Mowrer and Lamoreaux study, as well as others, produced widespread acceptance for the two-factor theory of avoidance learning.

About ten years later, however, Harvard psychologist Richard L. Solomon and his students, Lyman Wynne and Leon Kamin, obtained some results which did not fit Mowrer's theory very well. Their study—apparently conducted mainly to test the effectiveness of several extinction procedures—produced unexpected evidence suggesting that the two-factor theory was incomplete.

[3] The material in this section is based largely on R. L. Solomon, L. J. Kamin, and L. C. Wynne, "Traumatic Avoidance Learning: the Outcomes of Several Extinction Procedures with Dogs," *Journal of Abnormal and Social Psychology,"* IIL (1953), 291–302; and on R. L. Solomon and L. C. Wynne, "Traumatic Avoidance Learning: Acquisition in Normal Dogs," *Psychological Monographs*, LXVII, No. 354 (1953).

Although Solomon studied dogs instead of rats, the avoidance training procedure he used was very similar to that used by Mowrer and Lamoreaux.

First, Solomon and his collaborators made sure that their subjects didn't already have the habit that they were supposed to learn in the experiment. They led each dog into the experimental room on a leash and coaxed it into one of the two compartments of a large box. The box was similar to the one used by Mowrer and Lamoreaux, except that it had to be larger to hold the larger animals, and it was divided in two by a wall. This wall consisted of a barrier that was fixed at the height of the dog's back and, resting on top of that, a solid gate that could be lifted by the experimenter.

When the dog entered the box for the preliminary testing, both compartments were brightly lighted and the gate was down (closed). Then the experimenter stepped on a foot pedal which turned off the lights in the dog's compartment, and at the same time he pulled a cord which lifted the gate. He watched to see if the dog would jump over the barrier into the other, still lighted compartment. Any dog that jumped on any of the ten preliminary trials was excluded from the main part of the experiment.

Starting next day, the selected dogs were trained to jump over the barrier. This was done by making one addition to the previous procedure. Again the light went off and the gate lifted, but this time there was a strong shock from the steel floor ten seconds later. In attempting to escape the shock, the dog eventually scrambled over the barrier to the non-electrified side, and the gate closed behind it. On the next trial, the same procedure was repeated in the dog's present compartment.

As the trials passed and the dog jumped back and forth between the two compartments, the experimenter used a stopwatch to measure how soon the dog jumped after each "light out–gate up." Of course whenever this jumping time was less than ten seconds, the dog completely avoided the shock.

Sooner or later the dog would learn the avoidance response well enough for the main part of the experiment—the extinction procedures—to begin. But how much learning was enough? In an attempt to teach all the dogs exactly the same amount, Solomon used the same stopping point or criterion of learning for each one; when a dog had avoided the shock ten trials in a row, it was considered ready for the extinction procedure.

Then the learned avoidance response was attacked with several different procedures, two of which are described here. One of these was an "ordinary" extinction procedure: trials were continued exactly as before, except that the shock was permanently shut off. These dogs received ten trials a day for twenty days, with the experimenter continuing to time their jumps.

The "glass barrier" procedure likewise involved permanently shutting off the shock. In addition, when the gate was raised on the fourth, fifth, sixth, and seventh of each day's ten trials, there stood behind it a sturdy piece of glass which prevented the dog from jumping. The glass was made visible by three vertical strips of tape attached to it. Each of nine dogs was run 100 trials under this procedure; some of these dogs had previously completed the ordinary extinction procedure.

Solomon's results. The "ordinary" procedure failed to produce complete extinction in any of the thirteen dogs used, whereas the "glass barrier" procedure extinguished the avoidance response in two of the nine subjects. More interesting, perhaps, were several other results, all obtained in the ordinary extinction condition.

1. Despite the absence of shock, the dogs tended to jump sooner and sooner as the ordinary procedure continued until, toward the end of the 200 trials, the mean jump occurred only about 1.6 seconds after "light out–gate up." This probably would not surprise Mowrer, whose theory is that fear reduction continues to reinforce the avoidance response even if shock is avoided.

2. At the same time, the dogs showed less and less fear. That is, fear reactions such as drooling and pupil dilation occurred less frequently as jumping got faster and faster. Mowrer's theory would lead us to think that this meant the dogs' fear was extinguishing.

3. However, this steady decrease in fear could not have been extinction because later, when some of the same dogs were prevented from jumping by the glass barrier, they showed signs of strong fear. If their fear had been extinguished, they would not have been so afraid of the box. This finding didn't seem to fit Mowrer's two-factor theory very well.

4. If a dog happened to jump especially late on one extinction trial, even though it didn't receive a shock it jumped early on the next trial. This was discovered by inspecting the records of the individual dogs, and probably would have gone unnoticed if the investigators had followed the usual practice of looking only at the mean results for the entire group of subjects. This is a second finding not easily explained by the two-factor theory.

SOLOMON'S THEORY OF ANXIETY CONSERVATION[4]

Solomon and Wynne devised a theory which could account for all of the above findings. Their theory was based on the idea that it takes a certain

[4] The material in this section is based largely on R. L. Solomon and L. C. Wynne, "Traumatic Avoidance Learning: the Principles of Anxiety Conservation and Partial Irreversibility," *Psychological Review,* LXI (1954), 353–85.

amount of time—they estimated 1.5 to 2.5 seconds—for a conditioned fear response to build up to full strength after the occurrence of a conditioned stimulus such as "light out–gate up." In the above study, many jumps occurred sooner than this, thereby "conserving" the fear, that is, preventing it from reaching its peak. This theory helped to explain the above findings as follows:

1. Mowrer had theorized that avoidance extinction is delayed because it has to wait for fear to extinguish. But even this theory might not fully account for 200 unreinforced trials without any sign of extinction. Solomon added to Mowrer's theory the new idea that fear extinction is itself an unusually slow process, because of fear conservation. This new hypothesis was based on the rather widely accepted principle that the weaker the response that occurs on any unreinforced trial, the less the extinction that results from that trial.

2. The dogs showed less and less fear as the extinction procedure continued *because* they were jumping faster and faster. The faster they jumped, the weaker the fear response that had time to build up.

3. The dogs showed fear when prevented from jumping out of the compartment by the glass barrier because they had never stopped being afraid of the compartment. Although fear may have appeared permanently extinguished, actually it was simply not being given enough time to occur.

4. A dog that jumped late on one trial jumped quickly on the next because on the former trial a large amount of fear had time to build up, and therefore a large amount of reinforcement (that is, fear reduction) occurred when the jump finally did take place. If more reinforcement causes more learning, this large amount of fear reduction would produce a strong learned tendency to jump. This strong tendency would then produce a particularly rapid jump on the next trial.

11 Evaluation of the Mowrer and Solomon Experiments

There can be little doubt that the Mowrer and Solomon studies described in Chapter 10 had a worthwhile goal: to find out how fear and avoidance extinguish. If psychologists could learn how to make these responses extinguish rapidly, neurosis would lose most of its sting.

The first part of this chapter discusses the experimental techniques used in the Mowrer study and in the part of Solomon's study where different extinction procedures were tested. Solomon's unexpected results concerning the relationship between fear and jumping speed, being non-experimental in nature, are discussed separately in the last section of the chapter.

ACCURACY OF MEASUREMENT

Reliability. Mowrer and Solomon planned their experiments so that all the essential variables would lend themselves to highly objective measurement. Mowrer had only to observe whether a rat ran soon enough to avoid shock. Solomon, in the experimental part of his study, had only to measure how soon a dog jumped after the light went out and the gate went up. We certainly can have no doubts about the objectivity of these measurements.

As previously mentioned, the reliability of a mean tends to be higher, the more individual measurements have gone into that mean. Although neither Mowrer nor Solomon used a large number of subjects, for some variables they made up for it by taking many measurements on each subject—one measurement on each of the many trials. Mowrer measured avoidance on each of 100 trials and Solomon measured jumping speed on each of 200 ordinary extinction trials. These large numbers of measurements were probably partly responsible for the fact that the superiority of Mowrer's "simultaneous" group and the increase in jumping speed found by Solomon[1] were statistically significant.

Regarding another of Solomon's dependent variables—whether or not complete extinction occurred—only one measurement was available for each subject. While none of the thirteen "ordinary" extinction dogs showed complete extinction, two (22 per cent) of the nine "glass barrier" dogs did. Although a difference between 0 per cent and 22 per cent may look large, it is not statistically significant for this small a sample of subjects. Two things could have made this difference more reliable: a larger sample or a larger obtained difference.

Validity. It is difficult to reject Mowrer's assumption that the number of successful avoidance responses his rats made reflected the strength of their habit to avoid. Of course there are always other possibilities, but in this case none seems very likely. For example, strength of the motive to avoid could affect the number of avoidance responses that occur. But variables that could have caused differences in this motive, such as intensity of shock, were controlled. Furthermore, the one variable on which the groups did differ—the stopping point of the buzzer—doesn't seem capable of affecting the motive to avoid.

Similarly, it is difficult to imagine that Solomon's jumping-time scores or "extinction" scores could be anything other than valid measures of the strength of avoidance habit.

GENERALIZABILITY

Solomon, Kamin, and Wynne were optimistic about the generalizability of some aspects of their work. They wrote: "We feel that the order of events which we have described is general to all learned avoidance responses."[2] While this feeling may have been accurate, their study did not prove that it was—as they well knew.

---

[1] Although no mention was made of the significance of this result in the article by Solomon, Kamin, and Wynne, Solomon has written to me that the jumping times were longer on the first ten extinction trials than on the last ten and that this mean difference was significant at well beyond the .05 level.

[2] R. L. Solomon, L. J. Kamin, and L. C. Wynne, "Traumatic Avoidance Learning: the Outcomes of Several Extinction Procedures with Dogs," *Journal of Abnormal and Social Psychology*, IIL (1953), 299.

Regarding subjects, there is the question of whether the Mowrer and Solomon findings can be generalized to human neurotics. In fact, it is even a question whether the avoidance behavior of rats (studied by Mowrer) and that of dogs (studied by Solomon) are comparable. While psychologists don't yet know enough about interspecies differences to answer these two questions confidently, the recent finding that even different strains of rats may show statistically significant differences in avoidance learning is enough to make one doubtful.

Even if these problems were overcome, there would still remain the possibility that the stimulus situations used in these experiments differ too greatly from the situation typically facing the neurotic human to permit much generalization. For example, in both of these studies the subject could escape or avoid the shock only by going to a compartment where he had previously been shocked. This procedure of "shuttling" the animal back and forth, it has been found, results in much slower avoidance learning than a nonshuttle procedure—for example, one where the animal always escapes from compartment A to compartment B, never the reverse. It seems entirely possible that humans typically learn avoidances by a nonshuttle kind of procedure. If so, this might further limit the generalizability of these results to the human neurotic.

CAUSALITY

Relationships. Mowrer found a statistically significant relationship between the stopping point of the buzzer and the number of trials a rat succeeded in avoiding shock. Solomon obtained a nonsignificant relationship between the variable of ordinary versus glass barrier procedure, and the number of animals in which the learned avoidance response extinguished completely.

Control. Mowrer controlled several variables by holding them constant. For all his subjects he used the same training box, the same laboratory (soundproofed to keep it uniformly quiet), and the same shock and buzzer. Solomon, too, used this method of control: all his dogs were trained in the same box, according to the same procedure.

The designs of both studies allowed subjects to be used as their own controls for some comparisons but not for others. Both Mowrer and Solomon looked at trends in performance from trial to trial; since the same subjects performed on each trial, they served as their own controls. This type of control was of course not present when different groups of subjects, such as Mowrer's three training groups, were compared.

Mowrer matched his groups of rats on genetic strain and ratio of males to females. Solomon used matching when he measured the initial tendencies of his dogs to jump over the barrier and then assigned dogs having exactly the same score—zero jumps in ten trials—to the different groups.

Finally, although their reports do not mention this matter, it seems likely that Mowrer also used randomization to assign subjects to groups, and at least possible that Solomon did likewise.

Order. Since Mowrer manipulated the independent variable in his hypothesis—namely, time between the occurrence of the avoidance response and the stopping of the buzzer—he could be certain that this variable was causing the obtained differences in number of avoidance responses. Since Solomon determined which subjects would undergo the ordinary extinction procedure and which the glass barrier procedure, he could have been certain—if he had obtained a significant difference in the amount of extinction occurring in the two groups—that this difference in procedure caused the obtained difference in extinction. But since this extinction difference was not significant, it might very well have been due entirely to random error.

SERENDIPITOUS FINDINGS

If a researcher discovers something he was not looking for, his finding is said to be "serendipitous." It seems likely that Pavlov's discovery of "experimental neurosis" (see Chapter 8) was largely serendipitous. The same appears to be true of all of Solomon's findings described in Chapter 10, except the one upon which we have been concentrating so far in this chapter. The Pavlov and Solomon studies illustrate the fact that psychology does not always progress unerringly from the lesser certainty of the exploratory study to the greater certainty of the field and laboratory studies. Instead, relationships which previously have been overlooked sometimes pop up unexpectedly in field or laboratory studies which, of course, have not been planned to focus their best methods on them.

Apparently Solomon and his collaborators planned their research primarily to study the relationship between various extinction procedures and the amount of extinction produced. They brought most of the techniques of the laboratory experiment to bear upon this relationship. The independent variable (extinction procedure) was manipulated, extraneous variables were controlled, and the measurement of the dependent variable seems to have been quite adequate.

However, these experimenters seem to have been somewhat outflanked by the unexpected relationship between jumping speed and fear. At least they had made no provision for manipulating jumping speed, the independent variable in this relationship.

For this reason, Solomon's explanation of this relationship (the fear-conservation theory) probably did not have the certainty that is ordinarily afforded by experimentation. This does not mean that experimenters should ignore unexpected results; quite the contrary, it is often very worthwhile to pay attention to such results. Although Solomon's serendipitous findings would have to be confirmed by further studies focused directly upon those variables, they had the important result of suggesting a new and possibly valuable idea to supplement Mowrer's two-factor theory in explaining the stubborn persistence of learned avoidance behavior.

12

Wolpe Applies Learning Principles to the Treatment of Neurotics

Clearly psychological research since the time of Freud has produced new findings about anxiety. Shouldn't these findings permit modern psychologists and psychiatrists to understand and cure neurosis better than Freud was able to do? The fact is that some of the more recently discovered principles have been applied to neurosis, with results that seem promising. Several of these principles and their applications are discussed in this chapter.

ANXIETY CAN BE CONDITIONED[1]

Since the point that anxieties and phobias can be learned was made first and most forcefully for American psychologists by John Watson's and Rosalie Rayner's demonstration with young Albert, that study will be described first.

About 1920—seven years after he had "founded" behaviorism—Watson was at Johns Hopkins University, doing research on children. Searching

[1] The material in this section is based largely on J. B. Watson and Rosalie Rayner, "Conditioned Emotional Reactions," *Journal of Experimental Psychology*, III (1920), 1–14; and on J. B. and Rosalie R. Watson, "Studies on Infant Psychology," *The Scientific Monthly*, XIII (1921), 493–515.

for a child in whom he might demonstrate the classical conditioning of a fear response, Watson found 11-month-old Albert, who filled his requirements in two ways: first, Albert was relatively accessible, since he lived in a hospital, near his mother who was a wet nurse. Second, he was "stolid and unemotional"; in fact, he seemed afraid of nothing but loud noises. This made Watson feel confident that the fear conditioning procedure would not have any serious effects upon Albert. Many other psychologists, however, have doubted the ethicality of performing this experiment on any child, stolid or not.

The study was apparently conducted in a hospital darkroom which had been converted into a laboratory by lighting it and adding a table covered with a mattress.

First, before any conditioning, Watson and Rayner placed Albert on the mattress and presented to him such objects as a white rat, a rabbit, a Santa Claus mask, a seal fur coat, and cotton wool. None of these stimuli produced any fear.

Several days later, Albert was again placed on the mattress, and conditioning was begun. One experimenter stood in front of Albert, presenting stimuli to him, and the other waited behind Albert, holding a suspended steel bar in one hand and a hammer in the other. Watson described the first conditioning trial as follows:

> White rat suddenly taken from the basket and presented to Albert. He began to reach for the rat with left hand. Just as his hand touched the animal the bar was struck immediately behind his head. The infant jumped violently and fell forward, burying his face in the mattress. He did not cry, however.[2]

This procedure, which is diagrammed in Figure 6, was teaching Albert to fear the rat. This fact is indicated by his behavior when, after rat and noise had been paired seven times, the rat was presented once without the noise:

> The instant the rat was shown the baby began to cry. Almost instantly he turned sharply to the left, fell over on left side, raised himself on all fours and began to crawl away so rapidly that he was caught with difficulty before reaching the edge of the table.[3]

Several days later Watson and Rayner looked to see whether this newly acquired fear of rats would generalize to other, similar stimuli. When the rabbit was now presented, "he leaned as far away from the animal as possible, whimpered, then burst into tears." In reaction to the seal fur coat, he "withdrew immediately to the left side and began to fret."

[2] *Journal of Experimental Psychology*, III, 4.
[3] *Journal of Experimental Psychology*, III, 5.

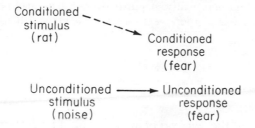

FIGURE 6 Watson and Rayner's classical conditioning with Albert.

As for the cotton wool, "he kicked it away but did not touch it with his hands." To the Santa Claus mask, "he was again pronouncedly negative." And when Watson lowered his own head to see if Albert would play with his prematurely white hair, "Albert was completely negative." Whereas none of these stimuli had produced fear before the conditioning, they did now, presumably because they were similar to the feared rat in being white and furlike. With his building blocks, however, Albert would still play without any hesitation.

Watson next wanted to know how long Albert's conditioned fears would last. Since neurotic fears are often long-lasting, if Albert's learned fears were of the same nature as neurotic fears, they too should be long-lasting. To find this out, Watson gave Albert no further conditioning for 31 days. At the end of this period, his reactions to the rat and the similar objects were again tested. He still showed some signs of fear to all of them. This finding strengthened Watson's belief that the fears of neurotic patients are originally acquired through classical conditioning.

The third of Watson's projects concerning Albert—an attempt to remove his conditioned fears—could not be carried out because Albert's mother removed him from the hospital. Watson wrote that if he had had the opportunity, he would have tried to substitute a positive response for the fearful one by (1) giving Albert food when the rat was presented, and by (2) letting him imitate other children who were not afraid of the animal. As will presently be seen, another experimenter did try out these two methods a short while later.

Watson had demonstrated to the satisfaction of many that at least some neurotic fears are learned. This notion appears to be contrary to some of Freud's ideas, as Watson himself implied when he mockingly predicted that, if Albert ever should undergo psychoanalysis for his fur phobia, the analyst would tease from him a dream showing this fear to be based on some sexual event in childhood. Furthermore:

> If the analyst has sufficiently prepared Albert to accept such a dream when found as an explanation of his avoiding tendencies, and if the analyst has

the authority and personality to put it over, Albert may be fully convinced that the dream was a true revealer of the factors which brought about the fear.[4]

HOW CAN ANXIETY BE REMOVED?[5]

Several ideas about the removal of anxiety might be derived from previous chapters. First, Freud's revised theory that it is anxiety that causes repression seems to imply that anxiety cannot be reduced merely by removing repression, but must somehow be attacked directly. This, in fact, is the position of Joseph Wolpe and the other behavior therapists, who will be discussed shortly.

How can the therapist attack anxiety directly? One alternative is to leave it alone; but a month's respite failed to remove Albert's phobia.

Another alternative is to try to extinguish the fear response; but fear ordinarily extinguishes slowly, if at all, as Mowrer and Solomon showed. One reason why fear extinguishes so slowly seems to be that it is difficult to present a feared stimulus to a subject for any length of time; he escapes or avoids it as quickly as he can, and this, according to Solomon, retards extinction.

This suggests a third alternative which might be more effective than either leaving the fear alone or attempting to extinguish it in the ordinary manner. The therapist might introduce an approach tendency that will counteract the avoidance tendency and thus keep the patient in the feared situation so that extinction can occur more rapidly. The approach tendency used should be strong enough to "overpower" or inhibit the avoidance tendency, as in the early part of Pavlov's experiment, when the tendency to eat the food was still inhibiting the tendency to escape the shock. In terms of the methods suggested by Watson, it would probably be advisable to begin with a strong tendency to eat, or to imitate fearless children, and a weak tendency to fear the phobic stimulus. This is essentially the idea that is used in the studies described in the rest of this chapter.

Probably the first to use this idea in therapy was Mary Cover Jones, a child psychologist then at Columbia University. Under Watson's guidance, she set out to finish the job Watson and Rayner had begun, by demonstrating the removal of fear. Upon testing children staying in a

[4] *Journal of Experimental Psychology*, III, 14.

[5] The material in this section is based largely on Mary C. Jones, "The Elimination of Children's Fears," *Journal of Experimental Psychology*, VII (1924), 382–90; and on Mary C. Jones, "A Laboratory Study of Fear: The Case of Peter," *Pedagogical Seminary* (now *Journal of Genetic Psychology*), XXXI (1924), 308–15.

child-care institution, Mrs. Jones found several who displayed unreasonable fears.

One of these children, three-year-old Peter, was afraid of rabbits, cotton, a fur coat, and a feathered hat. Although the source of these anxieties was not known, Mrs. Jones undoubtedly suspected that fear had been conditioned to one of these objects and then had generalized to the other, similar objects. The two main methods used to rid Peter of his anxieties were essentially those Watson had suggested earlier.

Throughout the first seven sessions of the study and from time to time after that, the "method of social imitation" was used. This method, which involved presenting the rabbit while Peter was playing in the laboratory room with other children who were unafraid of the animal, considerably reduced Peter's anxiety. Here is Mrs. Jones' description of one occasion when this method was used:

> Lawrence and Peter sitting near together in their high chairs eating candy. Rabbit in cage put down 12 feet away. Peter began to cry. Lawrence said, "Oh, rabbit." Clambered down, ran over and looked in the cage at him. Peter followed close and watched.[6]

One day shortly after the seventh session, Peter received a scare from a large dog and, apparently as a result, his fear of rabbits returned in full strength. Mrs. Jones decided that was a good opportunity to try out a different therapeutic method—"direct conditioning." Following Watson's earlier suggestion, she presented the rabbit while Peter was eating. On the first day this procedure was used, the eating response inhibited Peter's anxiety only when the rabbit was far away:

> Peter sitting in high chair, eating candy. E [the experimenter] entered room with a rabbit in an open meshed wire cage. The rabbit was placed on the table four feet from Peter, who immediately began to cry, insisting that the rabbit be taken away. Continued crying until the rabbit was put down 20 feet away. He then started again on the candy, but continued to fuss, "I want you to put Bunny outside."[7]

As direct conditioning continued, however, Peter allowed the rabbit to come closer and closer to him until, at the thirty-eighth direct conditioning session, he reacted to the rabbit as follows:

> Peter standing in high chair, looking out of the window. He inquired, "Where is the rabbit?" The rabbit was put down on the chair at Peter's feet. Peter patted, tried to pick him up, but finding the rabbit too heavy

[6] *Pedagogical Seminary*, XXXI, 313.
[7] *Journal of Experimental Psychology*, VII, 389.

asked the experimenter to help in lifting him to the window sill, where he played with him for several minutes.[8]

Not only had Peter ceased to fear the rabbit, he no longer showed fear of cotton, the fur coat, or the feathered hat.   Presumably, when the fear of rabbits was extinguished, this extinction generalized to the other, similar objects.

WOLPE USES THE INHIBITION METHOD WITH ADULT NEUROTICS[9]

Prior to 1944 Joseph Wolpe had firmly believed in the theories of Freud. In that year, Wolpe, then a military medical officer, found himself with the spare time to read a number of psychology books he had not read before.   In several of these he found evidence against Freud's theory of the Oedipus complex.   His faith in Freud shaken, Wolpe began studying the behavioristic psychologists, including Pavlov and Hull.   Eventually, through his experimental work at the University of Witwatersrand in the Union of South Africa and through his psychiatric practice, he developed a method for helping neurotic patients "unlearn" their anxiety.   This method, which Wolpe calls "psychotherapy by reciprocal inhibition," is basically similar to Mrs. Jones' method of direct conditioning.   However, it differs from her method in several ways which make it more useful with adult neurotics.   Like Mrs. Jones, Wolpe tries to produce in the patient a positive response tendency which will inhibit fear.   However, since he felt it was not always convenient to use eating, Wolpe explored the inhibitory power of a number of other responses.   While he found several that were useful in specific kinds of cases, the inhibitory response he found to be most widely applicable was relaxation.

Wolpe also differs from Mrs. Jones in his typical method of presenting the feared stimuli.   Although feared rabbits can easily be presented "in the flesh," this is less feasible in the case of large feared objects such as swimming pools, or buses, or horses.   To overcome this problem, Wolpe presents the feared stimulus, not in reality, but by asking the patient to imagine it clearly.

Wolpe's method of therapy generally includes the following steps:

1. The initial interview is conducted.
2. The patient constructs one or more fear hierarchies—lists of irrationally feared stimuli, arranged according to the amount of fear they produce.

[8] *Ibid.*

[9] The material in this section is based largely on J. Wolpe, *Psychotherapy by Reciprocal Inhibition* (Stanford, Calif.: Stanford University Press, 1958).

3. The patient, under hypnosis, is given practice in relaxation.

4. Therapy takes place: the therapist instructs the relaxed patient to imagine the stimuli he fears, beginning with the least feared and progressing gradually toward the most feared.

Each of these four steps will now be described at greater length. During the initial interviewing sessions, Wolpe sits at his desk, noncommittally taking notes on the history of the patient's symptoms and other aspects of his life. After history-taking, which may last one or several sessions, Wolpe gives the patient the Willoughby Personality Schedule (see Chapter 4). Next, typically, Wolpe explains to the patient that he is suffering from nonadaptive fear. He illustrates how such fear can be learned with the following story:

> "A young child goes into his mother's kitchen, puts his hand on the big, black stove and burns himself. . . . A lasting after-effect of this experience is that on subsequent occasions when the child enters the kitchen and sees the stove, he reacts with fear and with an impulse to keep away from it. . . . This, of course, is desirable.
> "But another, seemingly odd reaction may also be observed. Suppose that in the bedroom of the child's mother there is a large black chest of drawers. It may now be noticed that the child is also afraid of this chest of drawers, just because, in common with the stove, it has the characteristics of largeness and blackness. . . . Even in this limited example the disadvantages of such a useless fear may readily be seen. . . . If the chest of drawers should happen to be in the child's path, he has to make a detour. Finally, if his mother keeps candy in one of the drawers this is no longer accessible to him."[10]

The next step in reciprocal inhibition therapy is for the patient to compose one or more fear hierarchies. Some irrationally feared stimuli have probably already been revealed in the patient's history and in his answers to the Willoughby scale. The job of completing the list is given to the patient as homework. When all such stimuli have been listed, they are separated into their logically distinct categories, and the patient is asked to rank the stimuli in each category according to how much he fears them. One patient, for example, was bothered by fears about other persons being hostile toward her, fears about certain physical symptoms she had, and fears of funerals. With regard to funerals, she constructed the following fear hierarchy:

1. At a burial [most feared]
2. Seeing a burial assemblage from afar
3. Obituary notice of young person dying of heart attack

[10] Wolpe, *Psychotherapy by Reciprocal Inhibition*, pp. 111–12.

4. Driving past a cemetery

5. Seeing a funeral (the nearer the worse)

6. Passing a funeral home

7. Obituary notice of old person (worse if died of heart disease)

8. Inside a hospital

9. Seeing a hospital

10. Seeing an ambulance [least feared][11]

The other task Wolpe performs before starting therapy proper is to teach the patient to relax deeply. When it is possible, the patient is first hypnotized. Then he is instructed to tense the biceps, for example, paying close attention to this tension, and then gradually to relax them. This procedure is carried out for most of the muscles in the body.

When the patient is ready for therapy, he is hypnotized, instructed to relax, and asked to imagine specific items in his fear hierarchy, starting with the least feared items and working gradually toward the most feared ones. For example, once the woman who feared funerals was under hypnosis and relaxed, Wolpe said to her:

> "Now I am going to give you some scenes to imagine and you will imagine them very clearly and calmly. If, however, by any chance anything that you imagine disturbs you, you will at once indicate this to me by raising your left hand two or three inches. . . . Now imagine that you are reading the newspaper and that your eye falls upon the headline 'Prominent citizen dies at 86.' (*Pause of about 3 seconds.*) Stop imagining those words, and again concentrate on your muscles. Let them go completely. Enjoy this calm state."[12]

Notice that in this case Wolpe took a chance on starting, not with the least feared stimulus in the list, but at the obituary notice. While a strong fear response to this item could have had the undesirable effect of increasing the patient's fear of all the items, Wolpe guarded against this possibility by asking the patient to raise her hand if she felt anxiety coming on. If she had raised her hand, she would have immediately been told to clear the scene from her mind, and Wolpe would have started again, this time with a stimulus lower in the fear hierarchy.

We catch another glimpse of Wolpe's technique 16 sessions later, when he and the same patient had progressed up the hierarchy to "seeing a funeral." At this session, after hypnosis and relaxation had been induced, therapy proceeded as follows:

11 Wolpe, *Psychotherapy by Reciprocal Inhibition*, pp. 142–43.
12 Wolpe, *Psychotherapy by Reciprocal Inhibition*, p. 144.

"First, I want you to imagine that you are standing at a street corner and a funeral procession passes you. You may have some feeling of sadness, but apart from this you are absolutely calm. (*Brief pause.*) Stop the scene. (*Pause of about 4 seconds.*) Now I want you to imagine the same scene of the funeral passing in the street before you. (*Pause of 6 or 7 seconds.*) Now just relax. Think of nothing but your muscles. (*Pause of about 15 seconds*). Now I want you to imagine the same scene of the funeral again.[13]

On waking, the woman reported that she had been slightly disturbed by the first presentation of the funeral scene, less by the second, and not at all by the third.

EFFECTIVENESS OF WOLPE'S THERAPY

There are two questions that can be asked about the effectiveness of reciprocal inhibition therapy: (1) Is it more effective than no treatment at all? (2) Is it more effective than other methods of therapy, such as psychoanalysis? Some evidence on these questions will now be presented.

Compared to no therapy. Although it might appear at first glance that a method of therapy that produces any improvement is better than no therapy at all, this is not necessarily true. Some improvement might occur spontaneously. Unfortunately, no one has yet succeeded in getting a very trustworthy estimate of how much spontaneous improvement occurs in untreated neurotics.

Even if such estimates were available, comparing untreated neurotics with Wolpe's former patients would not be a foolproof way of discovering the effectiveness of reciprocal inhibition. Uncontrolled variables would make interpretation difficult. For example, if Wolpe's patients showed more improvement than untreated neurotics, it might be (1) because the neuroses of the former were less severe than those of the latter or (2) because Wolpe's preliminary training procedures, not the reciprocal inhibition itself, were doing the job.

An experiment[14] has been done which avoids these particular two problems. Peter J. Lang and A. David Lazovik, both at the University of Pittsburgh, found 24 college undergraduates who were greatly afraid of nonpoisonous snakes according to several measures. One measure was an observer's rating of how close the subject was able to come to picking up a

---

[13] Wolpe, *Psychotherapy by Reciprocal Inhibition*, pp. 145–46.

[14] P. J. Lang and A. D. Lazovik, "Experimental Desensitization of a Phobia," *Journal of Abnormal and Social Psychology*, LXVI (1963), 519–25.

harmless snake in the laboratory. We will call this variable "avoidance." A second measure was the subject's own rating of how afraid he felt when trying to pick up the snake. We will call this variable "fear."

These phobic subjects were randomly divided into an experimental and a control group. The control subjects received no special treatment. Each member of the experimental group received five private, 45-minute training sessions during which a twenty-item fear hierarchy was constructed, training in muscle relaxation was given, and hypnosis was introduced. Next, he received eleven private therapy sessions in which the feared items were presented as prescribed by Wolpe.

All the subjects' fear and avoidance of snakes were measured first at the beginning of the study, second after the preliminary training, third after the therapy sessions, and fourth—for the twenty subjects who were still available—six months after the experiment. This experimental design is summarized in Table 8.

TABLE 8   DESIGN OF LANG AND LAZOVIK EXPERIMENT*

Experimental group	Control group
First testing[a]	First testing[b]
Training	—
Second testing	Second testing
Therapy	—
Third testing	Third testing
6-months' interval	6-months' interval
Fourth testing	Fourth testing

* After P. J. Lang and A. D. Lazovik, "Experimental Desensitization of a Phobia," *Journal of Abnormal and Social Psychology,* LXVI (1963), 519–25.

[a] Only 8 of the 13 experimental subjects received the first testing.

[b] Only 5 of the 11 control subjects received the first testing.

The results of this experiment were as follows:

1. From the first to the second testing neither avoidance nor fear changed much in either group, indicating that the training was not having much effect by itself.

2. From the second to the third testing avoidance dropped significantly more for the experimental subjects than for the control subjects, indicating that therapy was superior to no therapy as far as this measure was concerned. Self-rated fear, in contrast, did not show any effects of therapy at that time.

3. Six months later, however, self-rated fear had further decreased in the experi-

mental group, indicating that therapy did produce significant, although more delayed, improvement on that measure also.

Why reciprocal inhibition therapy should have a more immediate effect upon persons' avoidance (as others see it) than upon their fear (as they themselves see it) was not explained by the investigators, but at least it eventually did have a significantly more beneficial effect than no therapy upon both of these measures.

Compared to other therapies. Now we put reciprocal inhibition therapy to a more difficult test; is it more effective than other available methods of therapy? Even if a particular therapy is better than nothing, it is not likely to be very widely used if an even more effective therapy is available.

Wolpe has categorized 210 of his former patients as (1) apparently cured, (2) much improved, (3) moderately improved, (4) slightly improved, or (5) unimproved. He found that 89.5 per cent of these patients were "apparently cured" or "much improved." For the same two categories, he also reported the means of the available Willoughby scores before and after treatment. These means are shown in Table 9. The finding that the Willoughby scores tended to decrease more for the "apparently cured" than for the "much improved" of course conforms to expectation. Since it does, it constitutes evidence for the construct validity of both the categories and the Willoughby scale itself.

TABLE 9   EFFECTS OF WOLPE'S THERAPY
ON WILLOUGHBY SCORE*

Classification of patient	Mean Willoughby score	
	Before treatment	After treatment
(1) Apparently cured[a]	45.2	12.3
(2) Much improved[b]	44.8	25.6

* After J. Wolpe, *Psychotherapy by Reciprocal Inhibition* (Stanford, Calif.: Stanford University Press, 1958), p. 218.

[a] Both before and after scores were available for 13 patients.

[b] Both before and after scores were available for 21 patients.

A comparable estimate of the effectiveness of one contrasting type of therapy—psychoanalysis—is also available.[15] Of 263 psychoanalytically treated cases gathered from several sources, about 63 per cent were judged to be apparently cured or much improved.

[15] R. P. Knight, "Evaluation of the Results of Psychoanalytic Therapy," *American Journal of Psychiatry*, IIC (1941), 434–46.

The estimate of 89.5 per cent apparently cured or much improved for Wolpe's therapy looks much better than the estimate of 63 per cent for Freudian therapy. Before jumping to any conclusions, however, we must remember the possibility of uncontrolled variables. For example, perhaps the patients who received psychoanalytic treatment suffered more severe problems and were therefore more difficult to treat than Wolpe's patients. There is also the possibility of inaccurate measurement—for example, perhaps Wolpe simply categorized more optimistically than the person who evaluated the psychoanalytic results.

Some of these difficulties were avoided in a well-controlled experiment on group therapy conducted by Arnold A. Lazarus, a behavior therapist.[16] In this study, 35 white, South African phobic patients were first classified by phobia. Then the patients in each class were randomly divided into two groups, one to be treated by reciprocal inhibition and the other to be treated by a combination of more traditional techniques. For each reciprocal inhibition group, Lazarus led all the members at once through the tasks of making up a common fear hierarchy, practicing relaxation, and finally, proceeding through the fear hierarchy while relaxed. This last step proceeded at the pace of the slowest group member. In the traditional therapy groups, Lazarus tried to maintain an atmosphere in which members would feel free to talk about whatever was bothering them, he encouraged patients to let off emotional "steam," and he ended each session with a summary and interpretation of the events of that session. In each pair of groups matched by phobia, therapy stopped in both groups when the reciprocal inhibition group had reached the end of its fear hierarchy.

After therapy was completed, its effectiveness was determined. For an acrophobic patient (one afraid of height) to be considered recovered, he had to be able to climb a fire escape to the third floor, then to take an elevator to a roof garden eight stories up, and finally to spend two minutes standing near the roof's edge, counting cars in the street below. For a claustrophobic patient (one afraid of being closed in) to be considered recovered, he had to be able to sit comfortably for five minutes in a closed room, with a screen standing a few inches in front of him. According to these criteria and others equally stringent for the other types of phobia, recovery occurred in thirteen of the eighteen patients treated by group reciprocal inhibition, but in none of the nine patients treated by the more traditional methods. Appropriate statistical tests show that this difference is clearly significant.

The evidence cited—while it is by no means complete—seems to indicate that reciprocal inhibition therapy produces more improvement than

[16] A. A. Lazarus, "Group Therapy of Phobic Disorders by Systematic Desensitization," *Journal of Abnormal and Social Psychology*, LXIII (1961), 504–10.

no therapy at all and, furthermore, more improvement than some kinds of traditional therapy, including psychoanalysis.

BREVITY OF THERAPY AND PERMANENCE OF RESULTS

Improvement is not the only criterion that can be used to evaluate a method of therapy. Other criteria are speed and permanence of whatever improvement occurs.

Wolpe's therapy seems to have a decided advantage over psychoanalytic therapy in terms of speed or brevity. Whereas psychoanalysis typically takes several hour-long sessions a week for one or more years, Wolpe's results of 89.5 per cent apparently cured or much improved were obtained with a mean of only 34 hour-long sessions.

Regarding permanence of improvement, psychoanalytic theory would lead us to expect Wolpe's methods to perform poorly. That is, a traditional psychoanalyst would probably argue that Wolpe treats only superficial symptoms, such as anxiety, and ignores the deeper causes, or repressed materials, which are the targets of psychoanalysis. According to this reasoning, once Wolpe removes one set of symptoms, the untouched deeper causes should produce a new set to take its place.

In hopes of showing this criticism to be groundless, Wolpe has tried to keep track of the conditions of his former patients. Of one group of 45 "apparently cured" or "much improved" persons whom Wolpe was able to check on from two to seven years after therapy, only one was found to have relapsed. This finding, which seems to contradict parts of Freudian theory, served to confirm Wolpe's doubts concerning that theory.

IMPLICATIONS FOR PSYCHOANALYSIS

Wolpe and other behavior therapists are highly critical of Freud's theories. In the first place, they contend that there is little evidence to support those theories in any unambiguous way: "After 60 years, . . . psychoanalytic theory still, in almost every particular, consists of nothing more than speculation. . . ."[17] Moreover, Wolpe claims, there is now evidence which contradicts crucial aspects of Freud's theory, especially his idea that repression is the basis of neurotic anxiety, and therefore the factor which must be removed in therapy. The contradicting evidence cited in this chapter is, in summary:

[17] J. Wolpe, "Psychotherapy: the Nonscientific Heritage and the New Science," *Behaviour Research and Therapy*, I (1963), 23–28.

1. Watson and Rayner demonstrated that something that looked very much like neurotic fear could be produced through classical conditioning alone. No repression was producing Albert's fear of white rats.

2. Wolpe's therapy is not meant to remove repression, yet there is at least some evidence that it is more effective than psychoanalysis. Wolpe has even suggested that whatever effectiveness psychoanalysis has might be due, not to the removal of repression, but to unintended reciprocal inhibition. That is, when a patient talks about his anxieties with the traditional therapist, the composure of the therapist may inhibit the patient's fear reactions in somewhat the same way that the presence of unafraid playmates made Peter less afraid of the rabbit in Mrs. Jones' demonstration.

3. The improvement produced by Wolpe's "superficial" therapy seems to be relatively permanent, in contradiction to the expectations of the traditional psychoanalyst.

In addition to criticizing Freudian theory in general, Wolpe has specifically criticized Freud's interpretation of the case of Little Hans (see Chapter 2).[18] Wolpe suggests that the incident of the falling horse, instead of being merely an "exciting cause," was probably the sole cause of Hans' neurosis. That single incident could have conditioned in Hans a fear of horses, particularly of horses that looked like the one which fell. If this simple explanation were accepted, Hans' Oedipal conflict, if such existed, would be judged irrelevant to his phobia, and Freud's attempts to cure Hans by removing the repression of this conflict would be considered useless. We have, indeed, come a long way since Freud!

[18] J. Wolpe and S. Rachman, "Psychoanalytic 'Evidence': A Critique Based on Freud's Case of Little Hans," *Journal of Nervous and Mental Disease,* CXXX (1960), 135–48.

13

Evaluation of Wolpe's Application of Learning Principles

The useful application of even an established theoretical principle often takes work. As we saw in the previous chapter, considerable research intervened between Mrs. Jones' test of the principle of reciprocal inhibition and Wolpe's achievement of a reciprocal inhibition therapy of general usefulness.

The applied psychologist often begins his work by modifying an available procedure to make it more practically useful. For example, Wolpe switched his emphasis from eating, which Mrs. Jones had used as the inhibitory response, to relaxation, because he found the latter more convenient in therapy. Also, instead of presenting the feared stimuli physically, Wolpe generally found it more useful to have the patient imagine them.

Of course Wolpe hoped that the reciprocal inhibition procedure, despite his modifications, would continue to reduce neurotic symptoms. But hoping is not enough. To be certain, it was necessary to gather evidence in the new, modified situation. What methods are best for gathering such evidence? Wolpe and a growing number of other clinicians believe that—contrary to clinical tradition—it is possible and desirable to test the effectiveness of psychological therapies with the most exact methods available. Because they made use of such methods, most of the studies described in the preceding chapter provide strong evidence for accuracy of measurement, causality, and generalizability, as we shall now see.

ACCURACY OF MEASUREMENT

To find out how effective his therapy is, the clinician needs instruments that will reliably and validly measure his patients' symptoms before and after treatment. In the studies described in the preceding chapter, several measures of neurotic symptoms were used. How reliable and valid were those measures?

Reliability. Lang and Lazovik measured students' avoidance of snakes by observing how close they could get to a harmless snake in the laboratory. Statistical tests showed that avoidance decreased significantly more for the experimental subjects than for the untreated control subjects, indicating that this difference was highly reliable. Also, by correlating the scores obtained on the first and second administrations of this measuring device, Lang and Lazovik showed that their measure had a reasonably high coefficient of test-retest reliability—0.63. These two administrations were considered comparable because the results made it clear that little of consequence had occurred in between.

Another measurement procedure was used by Wolpe when he categorized treated patients as apparently cured, much improved, and so forth. We have no evidence concerning the reliability of these categorizations, because no one has repeated the procedure to find out how consistent its results are.

Third, Wolpe used the Willoughby inventory to measure neuroticism. Thanks to the efforts of Willoughby, we can probably be quite confident of the reliability of this instrument.

Finally, Lazarus measured avoidance in phobic patients by putting them to realistic tests like standing on a tall building (for patients afraid of height) or sitting in a cramped room (for claustrophobic patients). Tests of statistical significance show that a reliably larger proportion of patients was cured by reciprocal inhibition than by the more traditional treatment. The reliability of the measuring instrument itself, however, was not checked.

Validity. It is difficult to doubt that Lang and Lazovik, by seeing how close a subject could get to a harmless snake, were measuring snake-avoidance. What else could this procedure possibly measure? Likewise, Lazarus could have been measuring nothing other than avoidance when he asked his patients to ascend the building or sit in the room.

What sound evidence do we have, though, that Wolpe was really measuring decrease in neurotic symptoms when he categorized patients? None, except for his finding that the Willoughby scores of his apparently cured patients had decreased more than those of his much improved patients. This relationship implies that if the Willoughby inventory is valid, these two categories must also have some validity. How much validity, however, we don't know.

The best evidence for the validity of the Willoughby inventory itself is probably Schotte's finding (see Chapter 4) that neurotic patients obtained higher scores on the Thurstone—the longer inventory from which Willoughby drew his items—than did normal persons.

GENERALIZABILITY

Since the whole purpose of the applied study is to find out what will work in some practical situation, it is essential that its findings be highly generalizable to that situation. Therefore it is an important virtue of these three studies that the stimuli, subjects, and responses used in them are, for the most part, very similar to those involved in the typical therapy situation.

To begin with, the therapeutic stimuli used in all three studies are probably quite typical of reciprocal inhibition therapy. Since this therapeutic method seems to vary relatively little from one practitioner to another, it is likely that even as few studies as this accurately represent the methods of many practitioners. In contrast, the method that Lazarus compared with reciprocal inhibition—his "traditional" therapy—is not highly representative of any widely practiced method.

The subjects used in these studies seem quite representative of neurotic adults in western cultures, where therapy is most often practiced. All of them were suffering neurotic symptoms, all were adults, and all lived in western countries. On the negative side, it may be worth noting that Lang and Lazovik, as well as Lazarus, restricted their attention to only one type of neurosis—the phobia; that Lang and Lazovik studied only college-age adults; and that Lazarus and Wolpe treated only white South Africans.

Finally, the anxiety and avoidance responses measured in these studies seem similar to the responses most therapists would probably be interested in. One possible exception is the response studied by Lang and Lazovik. Whereas they measured snake-avoidance at a time when subjects were in the laboratory with the experimenter, most therapists would probably be more concerned with their patients' phobic reactions at more typical moments.

CAUSALITY

It is not enough for the clinician to know that a treated group of patients improved; he also wants to find out whether the improvement was caused by his treatment. As we know, this calls for evidence regarding relationship, control, and order.

Relationships. All three studies under discussion showed a relationship between type of treatment used and amount of improvement shown. Subjects treated with reciprocal inhibition methods improved more than those not treated at all, in the Lang and Lazovik study; more than those treated by psychoanalysis, in the Wolpe study; and more than those treated by a combination of traditional methods, in the Lazarus study.

Control. Subject variables were perhaps the most important extraneous variables to control in these studies. For if different therapies are applied to groups that differ in the severity of their symptoms, in the extent to which they use their symptoms to gain sympathy, in the strength of their faith in the therapist, or in other ways, these subject differences alone might easily account for any differences in improvement. Happily, Lang and Lazovik, as well as Lazarus, were able to control all subject variables by assigning subjects to experimental and control groups in a random manner. In Wolpe's study, however, this could not be done.

Order. Because Wolpe's study failed to control subject variables and therefore offers little certainty that treatment and improvement had a direct causal relationship, there is no value in going on to ask which of these two variables was the first to show differences in his study. With regard to the other two studies, however, this question is well worth asking. In both of those cases, the answer clearly is that the difference in treatment must have preceded the difference in improvement and therefore must have caused it.

THE ACCUMULATION OF EVIDENCE

Taken separately, each of these three studies is vulnerable to criticism. This should not be surprising; it is virtually impossible to gather even reasonably complete evidence for accuracy of measurement, causality, and generalizability all in a single study.

   More convincing than a single study is a series of studies which produce similar results.   This is true, however, only if the studies in the series share no common weaknesses.   One possible weakness that is shared by the three studies we have been discussing is that their authors are all enthusiastic advocates of therapy by reciprocal inhibition.   While it is natural that researchers should study what they are most interested in, it is also a fact that an investigator's biases can distort his research in many ways—some of them so subtle as to be nearly undetectable to either himself or others.   For this and other reasons, despite the apparent strength of the collective evidence that reciprocal inhibition therapy is highly effective, there are undoubtedly many who remain unconvinced.

14 Conclusion

We have seen that repeated studies, involving a wide variety of research methods, have gradually forced anxiety to reveal some of its mysteries. The discoveries that were described in this book will now be summarized.

It was Freud who first took up the challenge of anxiety. His exploratory case studies produced at least three valuable questions, but only the beginnings of answers to them: (1) How are anxiety and conflict related? Freud showed little more than that they are related. (2) How are anxiety and avoidance (mental and physical) related? Freud's last idea on this topic was that anxiety causes mental avoidance (repression). (3) How can neurotic anxiety and avoidance be reduced? Freud tried to do this primarily by removing his patients' repressions.

Since Freud's time, others have sought to improve upon his answers to these questions. Pavlov brought us closer to an answer to the first question by showing that at least one kind of conflict can *cause* anxiety and other neurotic symptoms in dogs. It was Pavlov's use of the experimental method that enabled him to show this cause-effect relationship in such a convincing way.

In connection with the second question, Gurin, Veroff, and Feld showed, among other things, that Freud's patients are not the only persons who use mental avoidance to deal with anxiety-producing problems. They found that the average U.S. adult reports that he sometimes does much the same thing. It was these investigators' use of the nonexperimental survey method that allowed them to describe the average U.S. adult so accurately.

Now to the third and, for practical purposes, the most pressing question: What special techniques will remove neurotic anxiety and avoidance

quickly? Certainly special techniques are needed, because avoidance behavior ordinarily extinguishes very slowly. This is so, the experiments of
Mowrer and Solomon suggest, because avoidance cannot begin to extinguish until its companion, fear, has completed its own particularly slow
course of extinction. This analysis seems to indicate that it is the fear
which must be removed first. But how can this be done?

Neal Miller had a hunch about this. He thought that fear might be
quickly removed by first presenting to the "patient" a stimulus somewhat
different from the one he fears, then substituting stimuli that are more
and more similar to it.

The same idea underlies Wolpe's procedure, in reciprocal inhibition
therapy, of going through the items in the patient's fear hierarchy. However, Wolpe added the principle that the patient should be relaxed
throughout this procedure. Is the resulting method of therapy effective?
Both experimental and non-experimental studies—one of them using the
highly reliable and valid measure of anxiety developed by Willoughby—
seem to indicate that it is.

WHAT NEXT?

Because of this large amount of research done in the years between Freud
and Wolpe, it would be easy to think that Wolpe's method of therapy
must be, if not the last word, then at least better than psychoanalysis.

Satisfying though such neat conclusions may be, they are seldom completely warranted in psychological research. While it is possible that
Wolpe's theory and therapy are more adequate than Freud's in every way,
other, less tidy possibilities should also be kept in mind. For example,
consider the hypothesis that Wolpe's therapy is more effective with
neuroses based on classical conditioning, whereas Freud's is more effective
with neuroses based on repression.

Testing this hypothesis is one possible next step in investigating
anxiety. In order to emphasize that there is always more evidence to be
gathered, we shall conclude this book by planning a study which might
be done to test it.

The rationale for the hypothesis we wish to test goes something like
this. Freud originally thought neurosis was based on repression and he
developed psychoanalysis to treat this kind of neurosis. In contrast,
Wolpe seems to think that most neuroses, even if initiated by repression,
continue to exist primarily because of classical fear conditioning. He
developed reciprocal inhibition therapy to treat this kind of neurosis.
Now it is possible that both Freud and Wolpe were pushing a single
theory too far. That is, perhaps in reality some neuroses conform to

Freud's ideas, and others, to Wolpe's. If so, it is reasonable to suspect that each of these two kinds of therapy is most effective with the specific kind of neurosis for which it was developed. This line of reasoning, by the way, might lead us to guess that phobias—since several studies have shown them to respond well to reciprocal inhibition—are usually based on conditioning.

There are many therapies that could be applied in our study, and many kinds of neuroses they could be applied to; however, the first rule in planning a study is to keep it simple enough to manage. In this case, it seems most important to test the hypothesis that psychoanalytic therapy is more effective than reciprocal inhibition with neuroses based on repression. While this hypothesis may not be valid, at least it is clearcut enough that its validity can be tested.

To test this hypothesis, we would first need some subjects—say about 40 of them—who had neuroses clearly based on repression. One way to get them would be to try to identify persons already suffering such neuroses. However, it is difficult to probe the unconscious and such probing might remove the very repressions we were trying to find. Therefore let us turn to another possibility—namely, that of creating this kind of neurosis in normal subjects. Something like what we would need has been produced by hypnotizing non-neurotic volunteers, outlining to them a guilty act they have supposedly committed, and then bringing them out of the hypnotic trance. The result is an individual who is bothered by a guilty deed he cannot remember—exactly what we would want for our study.

If we decided to try this technique, we would need to obtain the services of an experienced hypnotist. As an added precaution, we would want to give the technique a preliminary tryout, to make sure it produced the desired effects without harm to subjects, before using it in the study.

If this first step proved practically and ethically feasible, the next problem would be to find therapists to administer some form of psycho-analytic treatment to half the subjects and some form of reciprocal inhibition therapy to the other half. One possibility here would be to enlist professional practitioners of both kinds of therapy. Another idea—probably more feasible—would be to recruit graduate students in clinical psychology and to brief some in a short version of psychoanalysis and others in techniques of reciprocal inhibition.

Finally, there arises the question of what we would want to measure in such a study. For one thing, we would certainly want to measure anxiety. The Willoughby inventory probably would not be very useful for this purpose because many of the symptoms mentioned there probably would not have had time to develop in our "artificial" neurotics. Probably our subjects would suffer little more than nervousness, which we could measure by asking them how nervous they felt, having observers rate how nervous they looked, or, best of all, using both of these measures at once. Another variable that might be interesting to measure would be the subject's ability to remember the "repressed" material after therapy. If reciprocal inhibition proved unexpectedly effective in removing these repressed neuroses, it would be helpful to know whether it had accomplished this feat by somehow removing repression.

There we have a rough design for a study. Now let's go through it once again, this time checking for accuracy of measurement, generalizability, and causality. This will allow us to polish the design a little more and at the same time will serve as a final review of these three basic issues of research.

ACCURACY OF MEASUREMENT

The subjects' ratings of their own anxiety will be used to illustrate this issue.

Suppose we decided to ask subjects the following question:

How nervous do you feel?   (Circle one.)
>   very nervous
>   quite nervous
>   slightly nervous
>   not nervous at all

One way to minimize errors of measurement would be to standardize this item by using exactly the same question, instruction, and scoring procedure for all subjects. Another way would be to increase the number of items in the test.

Now for estimating the reliability of our one-item test. Since no observer judgment is required in scoring, objectivity would obviously be high. Since no equivalent form is available, no coefficient of equivalence could be computed. And since the test is only one item long, no coefficient of internal consistency could be computed either. This leaves only stability. It would be easy to estimate stability if the measurements were to be applied to the same subjects twice with no therapy in between; the correlation between the two nervousness ratings would reflect the stability of this measure.

The only kinds of validity that would be relevant to this study are concurrent and construct validity. The former could be estimated by correlating the self-ratings of anxiety with the observer ratings of anxiety. We would have one piece of evidence for the construct validity of the self-rating measure if, in line with our expectations, it indicated less anxiety after psychoanalytic therapy than after reciprocal inhibition therapy. Content validity would not be needed here, since this measure would not be intended to represent some larger body of content such as that of a college course. Nor would predictive validity be needed, since this item would not be used to predict any future event.

GENERALIZABILITY

The situation to which we would probably most want to generalize the results of this study is that of actual therapy. Like many experimental studies, however, the one proposed here promises to have rather low generalizability.

To begin with, the stimulus situation used would differ considerably from the situation in actual therapy. Our graduate student therapists would differ from real therapists in their age, their training, and their commitment to the therapies used. The therapies themselves would differ from the genuine articles: the psychoanalytic method used would have to be much briefer than typical psychoanalysis, and they would not cost the "patients" anything.

Nor would our subjects comprise a random sample of neurotics under treatment. To mention some of their unrepresentative characteristics, our subjects would be hypnotizable volunteers suffering from relatively minor symptoms produced through hypnosis.

The responses measured, on the other hand, would not fare so poorly. If our measurement of anxiety were valid, we would be measuring something of prime concern to the clinical psychologist or psychiatrist.

CAUSALITY

If our "repressed neurotics" obtained lower anxiety scores after psychoanalytic treatment than after reciprocal inhibition, we could say there was a relationship between degree of anxiety and method of therapy.

To make sure that they did not influence this relationship, a number of extraneous variables would have to be controlled. The variable of the room used for therapy would be held constant—that is, the same room would be used for both types of therapy. It would be possible to use subjects as their own controls, but only if we implanted two "repressed neuroses" in each subject and treated one with the psychoanalytic method and the other with reciprocal inhibition. Groups would be matched on their mean anxiety before therapy. Finally, all other subject variables would be controlled through randomization.

As previously noted, this technique of control by randomization is one of the major advantages of the experimental method over the non-experimental one. This important safeguard can be used only when the independent variable is manipulated, not when it is varied through selection. Another major advantage of the experimental method is that it provides superior evidence for order. For example, if our two groups of subjects, whom randomization had made equivalent before therapy, showed differences in amount of improvement afterward, it would have to be that the difference in therapy preceded the difference in improvement and therefore caused it, instead of the reverse. This reasoning assumes, of course, that all influential extraneous variables were adequately controlled.

CONCLUSION

The study outlined above is only one of many that need to be done on the topic of anxiety and on every other topic in psychology. For our present understanding of behavior is like an unfinished jigsaw puzzle: several clusters of pieces have been fitted together, but most of the space is empty. Whenever the impression is given that the psychologist's knowledge is more complete than this, it is mainly because of the human tendency to focus on the islands of knowledge instead of on the oceans of ignorance between them.

This situation, while it may discourage some, should encourage others to use the methods outlined in this book to search for further secrets of behavior.

Selected Readings

Anderson, B. F., *The Psychology Experiment; An Introduction to the Scientific Method.* Belmont, Calif.: Wadsworth Publishing Company, Inc., 1966. (Paperback.)

Conant, J. B., *On Understanding Science.* New Haven: Yale University Press, 1947.

Hyman, R., *The Nature of Psychological Inquiry.* Englewood Cliffs, N.J.: Prentice-Hall, Inc., 1964. (Paperback.)

O'Neil, W. M., *An Introduction to Method in Psychology.* Carlton, Australia: Melbourne University Press, 1957.

Scott, W. A., and M. Wertheimer, *Introduction to Psychological Research.* New York: John Wiley & Sons, Inc., 1962.

Selltiz, Claire, Marie Jahoda, M. Deutsch, and S. W. Cook, *Research Methods in Social Relations* (rev. ed.). New York: Holt, Rinehart & Winston, Inc., 1959.

Index